Koontz

1985

From
Saigon to
Shalom

From Saigon to Shalom

The pilgrimage of a missionary in search of a more authentic mission.

James E. Metzler

Institute of Mennonite Studies (IMS)
Missionary Studies No. 11

HERALD PRESS
Scottdale, Pennsylvania
Kitchener, Ontario
1985

Library of Congress Cataloging in Publication Data

Metzler, James E.
    From Saigon to shalom.

    (Missionary studies ; no. 11)
    Bibliography: p.
    1. Missions—Vietnam.   2. Missions—Theory.
I. Title.   II. Series.
BV3310.M48   1985   266'.001   84-9313
ISBN 0-8361-3379-X (pbk.)

FROM SAIGON TO SHALOM
Copyright © 1985 by Herald Press, Scottdale, Pa. 15683
        Published simultaneously in Canada by Herald Press,
        Kitchener, Ont. N2G 4M5. All rights reserved.
Library of Congress Catalog Card Number: 84-9313
International Standard Book Number: 0-8361-3379-X
Printed in the United States of America
Design by Alice B. Shetler

90 89 88 87 86 85 10 9 8 7 6 5 4 3 2 1

to Rachel
    a faithful pilgrim companion

to Brian and Karen
    whose roots intertwine with the story

to our mission co-workers°
    for their caring support in times of searching

°James and Arlene Stauffer, 1957-75
Everett and Margaret Metzler, 1957-69
Luke and Mary Martin, 1962-75
Donald and Doris Sensenig, 1963-73
Luke and Dorothy Beidler, 1966-75

CONTENTS

Author's Preface — 9

PROLOGUE — 17

THE VIETNAM ENCOUNTER
  1. The Obvious Question: Where Have All the
     Missionaries Gone? — 25
  2. The Historical Question: What Chance Did
     U.S. Missions Have in Vietnam? — 30
  3. The Association Question: How Were U.S.
     Missions Seen in Vietnam? — 35
  4. The Worldwide Question: What Was the Impact of
     Vietnam on World Missions? — 44
  5. The Future Question: Will Missions
     Face Another "Vietnam"? — 51

SHALOM IS GOD'S MISSION
  6. The Vision: Upholding the Good Life — 57
  7. The Community: Creating Peoplehood
     Through Covenant — 65
  8. The Power: Living with God as King — 75
  9. The Wholeness: Finding Well-Being in
     Our Life Together — 87

SHALOM IS OUR MISSION TOO
10. Shalom Is Mission — 101
11. A Mission Shaped by Shalom — 118

EPILOGUE
Epilogue — 133
Notes — 135
The Author — 143
Missionary Study Series — 144

Author's Preface

This is a book in three parts:

Vietnam, the Problem. The first part examines the record of American missions in Vietnam, highlighting their entanglement with politics and war. From my own experience and observations, trying to tell it as I saw it, I pinpoint some of the questions confronting missions today.

Shalom, the Vision. The second section is a thematic study of the Scriptures, surveying the mission of God through the grid of shalom. It probes how God has been doing mission among the peoples of the world. This study reflects my struggle to reconceptualize the church's mission following my Vietnam sojourn.

Missions, the Application. The last section seeks to relate this paradigm of the divine mission to the concerns raised about the Vietnam experience. I make no attempt to offer simple solutions to the many facets of that confusing situation. But I do propose that the biblical vision of shalom, which was such a formative principle in God's mission, can give specific guidance for missions.

Some readers may become restless in the midsection, eager to see if any realistic options are suggested. You may skip the shalom study and go immediately to its application for missions. However, the vibrant power behind Jesus' identification of mission with shalom comes alive only as we catch the force of that driving vision of God through the eyes of the Hebrews. So I urge you to keep studying the original model in order to grasp what our Lord had in mind.

9

But why focus on Vietnam nearly a decade after U. S. missions have departed from that land? Actually, the concerns expressed here have been stirring within me for nearly two decades, and I would gladly have wished them away many times. The silence about that whole episode in mission history is so deadening that I doubted if anyone would be willing to resurrect the memories.

The new interest in Vietnam studies by students across university campuses is heartening. Increasingly, the youth who were infants during the peak of the U. S. involvement want to know what their fathers (and a few mothers) did in that far-off land. The thirteen-part TV series *VIETNAM: A Television History* shown last fall has reminded us of many unanswered questions. Might the youth in our churches begin to ask the same about their missions?

At the same time, the reports from Central America are a grim reminder that the problems we faced in Vietnam will not fade away like a bad dream. I hear the same agony from church workers now in this arena of strife. Sometimes it seems that nothing has changed, except the dates, places, and names.

But in the end, it was the affirmation and counsel from a circle of friends that encouraged me to finish the task: Willard Swartley, professor of New Testament and director of the Institute of Mennonite Studies; Wilbert Shenk, missiologist and director of overseas ministries for Mennonite Board of Missions; and LeRoy Friesen, director of peace studies at Associated Mennonite Biblical Seminaries.

I am grateful for the valuable suggestions of other friends who also read the manuscript: Luke and Mary Martin, co-workers in Vietnam; Alice and Robert Ramseyer, missionaries in Japan (Robert directs the Mission Training Center at AMBS); and David Augsburger, author and professor of pastoral counseling. I also gratefully acknowledge several church agencies which have given support to the project: Eastern Mennonite Board of Missions, Laurelville Mennonite Church Center, Mennonite Board of Missions, and Mennonite Central Committee.

These credits, which should include many of the teacher-writers named in the footnote to the dedication, symbolize the sense of peoplehood that has nurtured and anchored me in this pilgrimage. These, my shalom-people, have in great part laid the foundations for this study. The specific observations and applications—the context of blood, sweat, and tears—are my own embodiment of that nurture and teaching, for which I accept responsibility.

James E. Metzler
Goshen, Indiana
March 1984

From Saigon to Shalom

PROLOGUE

Prologue

An eerie silence greeted me as I stepped gingerly from our dining room into the back patio. Even the listless stars dotting the patch of sky between the protecting roofs looked strange in the fiery glow over the city. It was hard to believe that a bustling Asian city could ever be so quiet—no motors, no horns, no vendor calls, no voices. Only a dog raising its mournful cry in the distance. Such a deathlike hush. The whole city was gripped in a state of shock—four million people whose lives were filled with fear and confusion.

It was January 31, 1968. The night curtains had just been drawn in Saigon[1] on the first day of that unforgettable Tet. What should have been the most happy, festive day of the year had become a day of terror. Amid the bewilderment of unbelief and uncertainty churning in people's minds, one thing was obvious: Saigon would never be the same.

Just a few months earlier Rachel and I with two-year-old Brian had moved to Phu Tho, a suburb bordering the Chinese sector of the capital. It was the edge of a city bursting with refugees, and we were opening a new mission program in the area. We were living in a small apartment attached to the back of the owner's residence, connected with a door at our rear patio. Across the street out front was a long tree-lined wall surrounding the well-known Phu Tho racetrack for horse racing.

Our front gate was just a stone's throw from a major intersec-

tion leading into the city. Between us and the corner was a
medical laboratory for the South Vietnamese Army with a two-
story building along our courtyard. It wasn't a factor in our choice
of location, but the owner had pointed out that security would be
no problem with a military installation so close!

The first indication we had that this would be a day for the
history books came at 5:30 a.m. We had been sleeping only a few
hours. When rudely awakened by the sound of fireworks at the
lab next door, we mumbled about those eager soldiers who
couldn't wait to celebrate the Chinese New Year. Then some
louder explosions shook our bed . . . and we sprang to life with the
realization that it was rifle fire and mortars we were hearing—not
the usual string of firecrackers. We picked up Brian and huddled
against an inside wall for protection.

Just as dawn proclaimed a new day, the disturbance died
down. We began stirring in the kitchen for breakfast, causing the
owner to pop through the inside doorway. "There are Viet Cong
out in the street!" he blurted out in a tense whisper. He
repeatedly warned us to close all shutters and doors and to keep
out of sight.

His trembling reminded us that the warnings were for our
neighbors' sakes as much as ours. As northern Catholics who had
fled Hanoi in 1954 and now were accommodating Americans in
their apartment, they were in as much jeopardy as we. They had
seen streams of people quietly moving into the city during the
night, carrying NLF[2] flags and pulling carts with guns and am-
munition. Our landlord informed us that the lab next to our front
wall was in NLF control. Someone had counted eight bodies
including two American MPs (military police) lying in the
intersection.

I immediately thought of the sign hanging at our front gate
announcing an English Bible class for students. I had to assume
that our presence was known. So we prayed . . . committed ourselves to the Lord . . . and waited. I made sure that Vietnamese
copies of our mission's statement concerning the purpose of our
presence were handy. And I rehearsed a dozen times my "open-

ing lines" should the door burst open with visitors brandishing their AK47 guns.

Suddenly the owner's wife ran into the kitchen, saying that an American in civilian clothes had stopped his jeep in our driveway. He was hiding behind a tree along the racetrack wall. At that very moment we heard more gunshots from the intersection. My heart stood still as I envisioned one of our missionaries having come in our jeep station wagon to get us—killed in the attempt. I raced to their front door, only to realize in a glance that the man wasn't someone I knew. I stood dazed, watching him dash from tree to tree back up the street, wildly firing his pistol in the direction of the barking automatics.

I was stunned with the reality that the war was right outside the house. This time we were caught "behind the lines." How many more people were driving around without realizing that the NLF had dug-in positions controlling the boulevard? The radio playing soothing music and saying little was no help. I was terrified by the thought that our co-workers might be trying to reach us. But with no phone service in our area, I wouldn't risk someone else's life by trying to send a message. Again we could only commit it to the Lord. (We still did not know that the whole city including the U.S. embassy was under attack.)

Numbly we went about the job of preparing for the bombing and shooting that would surely come. Spotter planes were circling overhead to assess the situation and pinpoint positions. A house of tin roof, fiberboard ceiling, and tile-brick walls wasn't much protection for the battle that was brewing. We made a "bunker" out of four barrels in the back room. With our mosquito net draped over everything—a mattress on the floor, all available boards and mattresses on top of the barrels, candles, snacks, and tin-can urinal—this would be our refuge for the pending storm. The security provided was more psychological than physical, but it surely helped.

After a hasty lunch we packed suitcases with valuables and necessities—while the helicopters were swarming overhead. The air became electric as we tensed with dread at what was about to happen. The choppers opened up with machine guns and rockets for pass after pass over the intersection, while American tanks and troops moved slowly up the street. As we huddled together in our bunker, I faced stark, uncontrollable fear. With emotions already strained from the hours of suspense, I kept repeating Psalm 23 and the Lord's Prayer; but it did nothing to ease the trembling.

The terrifying din of war swirling around us defies description. The mini-cannons on the U.S. helicopters right overhead sounded like the worst gear-grinding noise one can imagine. This was punctuated by the hiss and explosion of the rockets they fired. Beneath that was the steady chatter of tanks and rifle fire. All around us bullets were popping, while fragments pinged on the tin roof and concrete courtyard. (Afterward I counted twelve holes in the side of the dormer above our room, several of them as large as a fist.)

Brian clung to his mother without a sound—in fact, he fell into a deep sleep, probably as close to being "scared to death" as one can be. I remember thinking that it was now our turn to taste what millions of the countryside peasants and villagers had been experiencing. We fully expected that the end had come for us as it had for countless thousands of them.

The raging battle crept along the street. But as the battle noise died down, we suddenly became aware of new crackling sounds. We heard a man shouting, "Chay nha kia!" ("That house is on fire!"). With sporadic gunshots still ringing, I ran to the window to open the shutter a crack. One of the rockets had hit a newly built house just two doors away—and across the back alley from a lumber shed. Neighbors formed a bucket brigade, and by courageous effort they were able to extinguish the flames. We did not need to flee into the streets! But farther away I could see billows of smoke erupting from large fires.

We then settled into a routine which was to continue for the next four days and nights. With roving bands of NLF forces in the city, everyone was edgy. Gunfire and strafing would burst out anytime and anywhere, sending us scurrying for the bunker. Sweaty GIs walked right through our apartment in their house-to-house search. The racetrack was used for a camp and munitions dump for resupplying the choppers—putting us right beside a tempting mortar target. Our district was one of the hardest-hit areas during the offensive, and fires burned stadium-sized holes in dense housing areas—one of them within a block of us.

It seemed safest for us to stay put. Electricity was off, and after two days we could get no more water. But we cooked our meat and rationed water to hold out a week. By day the streets and skies had lots of military action, but at night everything was still, everything except the alleyway behind us. During the night we could hear muffled tapping sounds on metal. Occasionally messengers would come and go stealthily. Several times a heavy cart was quietly pulled away. We also detected strange bird calls and became convinced that an NLF supply house was operating right behind us. We were indeed in a typical Vietnamese setting with divided loyalties all around us, which added to the tension and confusion.

That first night I recall glancing periodically at the stars to catch a bit of eternity, wondering if I would ever know a "normal life" again. The shattering events of the day had left as much debris in my heart and mind as in the street. The long, restless night was needed to sort through a maze of feelings. To calm the holy disturbance within us about the war, we missionaries had often quipped: "Just work—don't think!" Now this forced solitude allowed a flood of questions to pour in.

What bothered me most just then was the awful sense of fear that had gripped me that afternoon. Being confronted with the specter of death was not exactly a daily routine, yet I was quite dumbfounded at my reaction. Was I really that afraid to die? I wasn't expecting to give up life without some struggle, but I couldn't understand this terror that shook me to such depths.

Yet as I reflected on it, I knew that I desperately did not want to die in that way. It was my way of saying that my death—like life—must have some meaning. If a rocket had hit our house, we would have ended up as three more unfortunate casualties of the war. On the other hand, if the NLF had burst into the house with guns blazing, I would have been killed as a hated American. In either case I doubted if anyone would acknowledge my reasons for being in that place at that moment. Could any of our Vietnamese neighbors or friends believe that our presence was not related to the war or to our nation's policies and actions?

I concluded that night that I simply was not ready to die for a cause that I couldn't even believe in, much less support. Though I would continue to work and witness as best I could in that broken, bleeding land for two more years, I would never feel the same about being in Vietnam.

THE VIETNAM
ENCOUNTER

1

The Obvious Question

Where Have All the
Missionaries Gone?

We Were There

*I*n reflecting on the experience of American missions in Vietnam, one fact stands out most strikingly: Once we were there; now we are not. Of course, as with most statements made about that confused and complex struggle known as the Vietnam War, even this cannot be said categorically. Some mission agencies did not get involved directly. And not all have left totally, since a few groups continue to relate to Vietnam, though with drastically modified programs.

But in a general sense, the statement stands. Even a casual glance at the history for Vietnam in the *Mission Handbook*, comparing the tenth edition (1973) with the twelfth edition (1979), reveals a radical change that calls for explanation. During our nation's intervention in that land, American missions were there also in similar strength. Catholic and Protestant, evangelical and mainline, Church World Service and World Relief Commission, Baptists and Quakers, translators and nurses were all there in the thick of it. In 1973 twenty-six American mission organizations listed over 300 expatriates serving in South Vietnam.[1] Several organizations had fairly extensive programs, with the three largest groups having eighty-three, fifty-seven, and forty foreign staff members listed. Only a few of them had worked in Vietnam prior to America's involvement in 1954, while a good number of them were in the country only ten years or less.

Yet almost overnight nearly all 300 were gone. For some, "the end" came so suddenly that they barely had time to pack their bags, though it is hard to believe that anyone was totally unprepared. Many said a reluctant farewell to a decade of diligent work; for some it was the investment of a major portion of their lives. These 300 were not in Vietnam for venture or gain; they had been sent by the church and most would have acknowledged being called of God. Their devotion to the task had withstood the hardships and perils of the war year after year.

So Why Leave?

This is a haunting question. Why did we go? What made every mission suddenly pull out? Who made us flee, with many getting caught up in that tragic, nightmare evacuation? Did someone order us all to abandon our homes . . . our projects . . . our young believers and churches . . . our call? What would force a mission to desert its ministry of sixty-four years, the field of primary interest from its beginning?

One wonders how historians in the next century will view this 1975 exodus. Will this event not stand in marked contrast to the courageous confrontation of hostile governments and menacing colonialists by the missionaries of earlier centuries? We can't even say that our missions were expelled, ordered out, or definitely threatened in any official way. Most missionaries didn't stay around long enough to find out what the new government would do.

A handful of missionaries were captured by the NLF forces in the central highlands. While they suffered a great deal in the jungle along with their captors, the new government released them without deliberate ill-treatment.[2] On the other hand, a few chose to stay, observing the change of government and society while relating freely with their Vietnamese friends. They traveled, worshiped, taught, and baptized for more than a year beyond May 1, 1975. Their story, written by one of them, documents a radically different understanding, spirit, and attitude towards both the people and the conflict engulfing them than shown by most mission staff. Like the four young men in the fiery furnace, refusing to bend to the spirit of fear or defiance about them, these four youth demonstrated to the worldwide church that there was another way.[3]

Yet, the fact that confronts us is that missions were as entangled as the other groups of Americans in that chaotic rush out-of-country. How is one to view such an end? The U.S. government, military, and business world viewed their departures as disgrace, failure, and loss. Vietnam had proven to be the quagmire for their policies and strategies that many analysts had already sensed a decade before. Should the missions, then, which became identified to some extent with that cause, be seen any differently? Was the Vietnam experience a defeat and setback for U.S. missions as surely as it was for U.S. political and military forces?[4]

I would like to believe that missions should be as concerned for Vietnam today as twenty years ago, that God has not lost interest in the Vietnamese or even willed for our missions to cease witnessing among them, and that May 1, 1975, had no effect on Christ's loving desire to be with his people there through his body, the worldwide church.

If these assumptions reflect God's perspectives, it seems important to ask if our missions needed to close as they did. Isn't it proper to ponder if that mission could have been carried out those last two decades in such a way that both programs and people would have continued with only a minimum of disruption to assure physical safety during the final clashes? Why didn't at least one mission stay until declared *non gratis* or expelled? Was the overwhelming presumption that we weren't wanted based on phobia, fear, or guilt by association? The sudden flight of nearly all missionaries with all the other Americans may reveal more about us than about the new government.

One can make a case that in 1975 missions were reflecting lessons learned in the China episode twenty-five years earlier. We knew that our presence could be an embarrassment to local Christians and a hindrance to the national church. Such concern must be recognized, of course. But surely we can learn more from missions' vast and costly experience in China than when to flee.

Most distressing has been the strange silence in mission circles about the whole ordeal. Vietnam seems to have dropped out of mind and sight for missions just as completely as for the rest of America which wants to forget the traumatic episode. A glance through the mission publications of the mid-seventies shows how suddenly our concern for Vietnam vanished. The record suggests that American missions see the Vietnam interlude in the same way as the American government and people saw it—a chapter to forget.

Are We Accountable?

In the 1980s missions can no longer afford to ignore the Vietnam record. The Vietnam experience merits more critical review and analysis; hard questions must be asked and vital issues faced in order to avoid repeating mistakes. Perhaps we fear that the record tells the world more about the loyalties, the motivations, and the world-view of American missionaries than we care to admit.

We give the impression that missions find it difficult to be self-critical. Our primary interest seems to be in seeking out and exploiting the "open doors," without much awareness of why doors open and close and the role we play in it. I have heard China missionaries say simply that "the Lord of history" closed the door. That sounds irresponsible if there is any chance that the associations and attitudes of mission workers may have provoked the reactions that slammed the door shut.

It is not surprising, given how deeply and traumatically we feel about the subject, that we hesitate to think critically of our Vietnam experience. Yet it is hard to imagine any enterprise in our world today walking away from such an investment of people and funds:

> —without full disclosure of what objectives were met, left incomplete, or totally unrealized.

—with no official evaluation or analysis of why the program was
  terminated prematurely.
—with no accountability for the millions of hours and dollars spent
  in pursuit of those interrupted goals.

In my survey, only one out of four of the larger groups indi-
cated that they had undertaken a formal review or evaluation of
their total program in Vietnam.[5] One agency said that they planned
to evaluate what they did and how well it was done by observing how
successfully the members they left are coping with the new govern-
mental form and obvious restrictions.

But who will prod our vision with what might have been—
instead of monitoring simply what is? Such a drastic disruption is
an inviting opportunity to reflect and dream. Here is an occasion
to project how other approaches, patterns, structures, and
priorities might have established a church with different positions,
attitudes, and resources.

2

The Historical Question
What Chance Did U.S. Missions Have in Vietnam?

*I*f any of you are not ashamed for what your country is doing here, you might as well go home right now. You will never do my people any good."

These stinging words were spoken to a gathering of mission and relief workers in 1966 by a Vietnamese Christian who had just visited her hometown. Since this woman was a graduate of a U.S. college and was serving in Europe, we thought she might be more direct with us in sharing how her people felt. In keeping with her culture, she hesitated gently for some time. But after some urging, she leveled with unforgettable bluntness and emotion.

If the U.S. missions could have been set into a time vacuum in Vietnam, things would have looked quite different. But Vietnam was a grandchild of Asian nationalisms, with the grandparents of India, China, and Japan looking on with a knowing eye. In my worse moments during the '60s, I felt that Vietnam was as much of a snare for our missions as it was for our politicians and generals.

Why Did We Go?
It was quite a jolt to my spiritual ego when it first dawned on me that I was very much a child of the Kennedy Era. When I set out in 1962 to make my mark on the world, I went with full

assurance that God had called me. My church confirmed that call by commissioning me to go to Vietnam. I would have been unhappy with any suggestion that my spirit was akin to that of the Peace Corps—and quite disturbed about any resemblance to the clandestine Green Berets.

But I now recognize the same cocky attitude of having the answers for the world. For twenty years America had dominated that world, and Americans were looking for the next place to apply their magic. The Kennedy spirit was stirring us all to do our part in solving the world's ills. The little "undeveloped" country of Vietnam looked like a made-to-order setting to prove that all the needs of the world can be erased with an ample dose of applied Americanism. Of course, that was before Selma, Dallas, My Lai, Watts, Hue, Kent State, and Watergate had tempered our spirit with a tinge of humility and finitude.

This description of my outlook does not fit all missionaries. Yet, chu.ches and missions are comprised of people, and people reflect the cultural atmosphere and political tones of their time and setting. So it should be no surprise if the Kennedy-Johnson-Nixon expansionist style of the American ethos was reflected by the Vietnam missions—mixed with the traditional motivations for missions, of course. The main problem was that it played right into some strong images and expectations of the Vietnamese people.

Did that sudden burst of interest in Vietnam among U.S. missions just happen to coincide with our foreign policy development? Our pleas that we were "nonpolitical" were made in the context of some hard realities both in America and in Vietnam. When the United States began replacing France following the French defeat at Dien Bien Phu in 1954, only two Protestant missions were in the country. Less than twenty years later twenty-five Protestant agencies were there with nearly 290 people.

This is no attempt to resurrect the guilt trips of the '60s; and the point is missed if it sounds simply like another put-down of America. The concern is for missions, not America. The question is whether evangelical missions of the late twentieth century were not as entangled in expansionist policies and manipulative politics in Vietnam as in the colonial era.

The forms and methods of *Pax Americana* may show more finesse than with former ruling powers, but it still came across to many Asian peoples as new chapters of *The Ugly American*. Our missions had a crucial image-problem in that setting right from the start. And we seemingly allowed the swirling developments of national interests to carry us into an inescapable bind. I suspect that Christian missions became just as American as nearly everything else brought into that country during that decade.

A Specific Historical Context

Even a casual acquaintance with Vietnamese history should have alerted us that France was Vietnam's window for perceiving the Western world and Christianity. French missions had been operating strong programs since 1615. Through the centuries they became involved with internal power struggles between dynasties. Such meddling led to persecution by the more nationalistic emperors. By the mid-nineteenth century the Society of Foreign Missions was appealing to Paris for protection. Warships were sent to rescue imprisoned missionaries. On occasion they were released only after French warships steamed into harbors.[1]

The subsequent conquest of Indochina for subjugation as a colony of France was both instigated and firmly supported by Catholic missions. This was done to a people who glory in their ancient heritage as a society and nation—especially in their millennium-old struggle against the Chinese. Christians had won "the right" to propagate their faith freely by resorting to the sword and the scepter. All this happened only a century prior to the U.S. encounter.

What followed was a hundred years of deeply resented foreign rule perpetuated by the bonding of Christian missions and colonial interests. The resistance movement against this dual arm of church and state was often led by Buddhist monks.[2] The minority who embraced the new religion were often seen by their neighbors as acting in "pursuit of their self-interests" or seeking protection and assistance. Going to see the priest was the surest path to obtain some favor or action. And after communism became the predominant ideology in the resistance forces, becoming a Christian was one of the safest ways to avoid suspicion or being labeled as Viet Minh or Viet Cong.

Of course, that is all history. And Americans in general have never seemed too concerned or even interested in the historical roots or the cultural settings of the Vietnamese struggle. The U.S. presidents have insisted the broken treaties and promises of the past had little to do with the present. The problem with such a stance is that the American people never could understand why the spirit of nationalism always burned brighter on "the other side." The U.S. seemingly felt that such details could be ignored and is still bewildered and frustrated to know why its "brightest and best" couldn't do the job.[3]

The question here is whether the missions operated with the same attitudes and assumptions. Were we more knowledgeable of the setting and more observant of "the prevailing winds" that determined the outcome? I recall my surprise during furlough in 1967 upon meeting scholars and students on U.S. campuses who had a clearer grasp of what was happening in Vietnam than I did. I learned anew the proverb about living among the trees without ever perceiving the forest (and vice versa). Going to a people, learning their language, and living among them does not make one an expert on the whole.

Perhaps we did rush in where angels would have feared to tread. A vocal minority, Christian and pro-West, furnished support for our aspirations just as they did for Washington's interests. So we moved in, fitting in quite nicely with the expectations of both sides in the conflict. They saw American diplomats, advisers, military, businesses, and missions merely replacing the French of the past century.

America: A Protestant Nation

A striking but tenacious belief that I encountered early in Vietnam was that I represented a Protestant country. "America is

Protestant just like France is Catholic," my students repeatedly affirmed. It seemed only natural to them to expect a flood of Protestant agencies, missionaries, and interests. Why shouldn't the churches in America want to support and assist their country in its new venture and commitment as French Catholics had done?

The rub comes in the realization that American missions were seen as filling the same roles as their French predecessors. Only now the support was coming from Washington, the directives from the CIA, the information gathered for the U.S. Embassy, the protection supplied by the Marines. And one should now join the Protestants for the same reasons that the Catholic Church had looked appealing in the past century. The roles were firmly fixed before we even stepped onto Vietnamese soil.

Some of us were plagued with the awareness that after years of close association our Vietnamese Christian friends still believed that at least some of these connections were true for all missionaries. Did anyone really believe the missions' *profession* of being nonpolitical? Like the bamboo "bending with the wind," the Vietnamese can adapt in religion as well as politics. Their resilience and longevity as a people makes them willing to check out or endure anything for a time. They believe that they will outlive it and use the best from it. So when America dominates, become American; when communism prevails, adjust to it. Life itself is more precious than ideology.

These popular assumptions held by the Vietnamese are the background against which we must view the ways our missions and the war effort intersected. If the cause to which we were linked had been respected by the majority, and the way it was pursued had been acceptable to them, then perhaps we could have ignored such associations without serious consequence. But the balance tipped as the land became devastated, the people demoralized, and the nation destroyed. Missions were caught in a no-win situation. We had cast our lot with a system and a cause, and when they were gone, we were gone.

3

The Association Question
*How Were U.S. Missions
Seen in Vietnam?*

A joke made the rounds in Saigon in the '60s: Two villagers were eyeing the American who came into their hamlet speaking Vietnamese. Said one to the other, "Well, one thing we know for sure . . . he's either a missionary or a CIA agent—or both!"

Missionary Attitudes and Associations
To my knowledge, all missions (except USOM—United States Operations Mission) claimed to be nonpolitical. I believe that most if not all 300 mission expatriates would have disavowed any political connections or actions. In fact, when a few missionaries became so disturbed about the situation that they felt constrained to express their concern and dissociation from the war policy and strategy, their actions caused a stir in the mission community. That was viewed as political involvement.

On the other hand, many missionaries left no doubt that their support and loyalties rested with the USA. Increasingly, the war became the overriding concern and cause to which all other plans and objectives had to be subjected. The Tet offensive of 1968 made certain that even the missions isolated in the well-protected urban centers could no longer ignore what was happening all around them.

So one dominating topic of conversation persisted whenever

missionaries got together. There was often a sense of excitement and intrigue in swapping the latest reports and rumors (the two were mixed so easily) and in anticipating the next move. Usually only a few comments were needed to indicate where a person stood, what was the focus of concern, and how deeply it was felt.

Thus, in that context of civil dissension where everyone's feelers worked overtime, the Vietnamese had little trouble "reading" most Americans. In contrast to the sophisticated intrigues of the Vietnamese, who were always looking for double meanings and face-saving evasions, we Americans appeared rather open and naive—like the veteran missionary I heard insisting that America never uses propaganda; "Only the communists use propaganda."

For me to suggest or document to what extent U.S. missionaries were used directly in the war effort is impossible. Some individuals reportedly gathered or passed on information to security officers. I know that in the highlands some missionaries helped to organize civil defense camps for the highland villagers, and thus worked with provincial security agents to get weapons and uniforms for "our people" to defend themselves. In many situations missionaries and USOM advisers or military staff worked together closely.

Certainly on the level of social interaction there were many open, fraternal relationships. Mission workers traveled everywhere in military and government vehicles and aircraft. Some frequented bases where only Americans could appear—with special passes and military currency—at the club and commissary settings including restaurants, movies, tennis courts, libraries, and worship services. So many U.S. government workers, security advisers, and embassy people were moving about the country freely without military markings that it became quite confusing. I recall the surprise of a missionary friend upon learning that the nice chap with whom he regularly had been playing tennis was a CIA agent.

Moreover, many Christian agency staff didn't hesitate to verbalize strong support for the Saigon government and U.S. policy. They were equally ready to voice forceful opposition against the communists—meaning all opposition forces, of course. In fact, one could hear voiced in mission circles expressions of impatience that the U.S. policy was holding back its military forces.

I will not forget the day I tried to share some concern for the civilian casualties and suffering caused by the ferocious bombing in North Vietnam, concerns often expressed by students in my classes. With a puzzled look in my direction, my missionary friend replied, "Well, I really don't understand why the president doesn't wipe Hanoi off the map. That's what he should do to teach those communists a lesson." I glanced around quickly to see if any members of his youth group had heard him, then realized in chagrin that his attitudes were showing every day.

A Specific Example

As anyone can observe from the impact of Tom Dooley's writings, missionaries certainly did their share of arousing a war spirit back in the States by their letters, articles, and books. It is difficult to sense in many releases from the evangelical press any deeper or more sympathetic understanding of the conflict than would have come from the Pentagon. In fact, it is uncanny to observe how often secular reporters and analysts sounded more compassionate and prophetic than the missions.

I hesitate to mention names, as I have no personal vendetta. Yet some concrete evidence for these allegations seems required. So I will use a source that can be readily checked: a book on Vietnam mission work written by a long-term missionary and published by Zondervan Press.[1]

The book, entitled *Victory in Vietnam*, closes with a news-flash type epilogue of three pages, describing an attack on the home of one of their missionaries near the 17th Parallel. The house was blown up while the family was sleeping. All were seriously injured by shrapnel and burns. They had been flown to the U.S. Army hospital where they were recovering.

This wounded missionary had just written an article about three Christian tribesmen near their village who had been captured by the NLF forces. He wrote:

>They have been counted worthy to suffer for Christ and will enjoy the Savior's reward. The challenge comes to us: Can we match their sacrifices? Will we let atheistic Communism swallow up the 400,000 tribespeople of Central Vietnam and the missions of Vietnamese people here, while we casually sing "The Whole Wide World for Jesus!" No! We must match sacrifice for sacrifice!

The author then assured the readers in a final paragraph that this missionary was living out his challenge:

>[They] had been doing a fine work among the Baru—speaking the tribal language fluently, *preaching in the strategic hamlet villages* and ministering a great deal to the sick. *They were helping to make the Strategic Hamlet program a success* in the Cam Phu area and *this was hindering the Communists* in their great desire to destroy this hamlet program. Can we, too, "match their sacrifice?" (italics mine).

I have identified the mixed signals since you would not likely catch their significance if you have not been to Vietnam. But few Vietnamese would overlook them. Everything I know about the Strategic Hamlet project suggests that it was a colossal failure. It was a hated and despised control device which played a major role in the overthrow of the Diem regime. Having people settled in permanent, accessible locations where they had to return each evening was a highly desirable prospect for the missions' interests. But the means to that end were vigorously opposed, as were all those associated with the project.

So from the perspective of those Vietnamese they were "hindering," were these missionaries nearly martyred for their faith in Christ? Or were they seen as political agents inducing the people to accept a government scheme while claiming to minister to them? It would seem that if "helping to make the Strategic Hamlet program a success" was viewed as a vital part of *Victory in Vietnam*, then that same participation could be seen equally as contributing to the "failure" in Vietnam.

Such a collaboration and confusion cannot help but implicate the universal kingdom of our Lord. One can find such mixtures repeatedly in Smith's book: choosing the freshly vacated French military police billet for their mission headquarters, their son bringing "high American government and military officials from Saigon" for huge hunting expeditions involving many villagers, being flown to their mission outposts "by American military friends" when road travel was too dangerous, using the Marines to help build and support their orphanage, and so on.

Relating to Christian GIs

The last two items listed above deserve more attention: the interest of U.S. military people in relating to and assisting in missions. For some soldiers the chance to visit an orphanage, assist in a medical-dental clinic, or help in some construction project was a constructive way to use available time and resources, to say nothing of atoning for their involvement in killing and destruction. But more than that, many American GIs were devoted church members who wanted to use this opportunity to see and support a live foreign mission program.

Missionaries usually seemed pleased with the attention, help, and resources from the military. The friendly relationships with these "other Americans" eased the hardships and brought many stateside comforts to many "poor missionaries." In more isolated areas the missionary sometimes served as chaplain to the troops. And the interest in missions was taken seriously. I remember one missionary saying that he never took a preaching tour out to the villages without taking several GIs along. Another missionary called the Christians in the U.S. military today's largest untapped source of mission potential.

I don't know any easy solutions to this duplicity of major proportions. It was sadly true that the missionary was often the only bridge by which the military could encounter and appreciate the Vietnamese people in their normal setting and culture. But what were villagers to think if the GIs they saw building a chapel for the mission one day had torched their homes in a "search and destroy mission" the day before? How were they to feel watching these foreigners playing with the kids at the orphanage if they knew the mothers of the children had been gunned down in their gardens by strafing helicopters from the same base? These were daily occurrences. And such partnership helped to seal the fate of the missions with the military.

Helping with the Other War

This dual nature of the U.S. war strategy was distressing for those missionaries who did not want to be tied to or used by either side. The policy was quite honestly called The Pacification Program or WHAM—"Winning the Hearts and Minds" of the people. It was also dubbed "the other war," recognizing the political aspects of a civil revolution which simply cannot be won by military might.

The assumption behind this fundamental policy was that one can destroy and build at the same time. It required both pacifists and soldiers who would work together to offer a better life while dealing death to those who would not accept the offer. We often heard military and security advisers reminded that top priority must be given to winning the people over—that the war would be won or lost on the shift of loyalties.[2]

The pacification program was crucial to the matter of missions' identity, for it meant that social services and good relationships were as vital to the cause of the war as were weapons and battles. So church, government, and even military forces were all engaged in similar activities. At times they worked together as partners. The military created the refugees by their operations (often saying prior to the operation how many to expect) and asked the mission agency to care for them—to pacify them quite literally. So all the relief and development work we did clearly was of political importance—making the war that much more tolerable.[3]

Thus, in a civil conflict as in Vietnam, even a missionary's presence can be a useful tool. Being a good neighbor and a sympathetic American built attractive images and fostered support for the nation's goals—countering the repulsive images created by the devastation and death caused by other Americans. Even evangelism and church planting were supportive to the government's cause, since most people on both sides assumed that becoming a

Christian meant that one was also pro-West. That is why few Vietnamese could believe that any American would come to their country at such a time and not be involved in "the cause," despite all disclaimers.

In the intensity and tension of such strife, everything that a person is, says, and does becomes part of the struggle. And it is viewed as benefiting one side or the other. War, of course, is based on taking sides and refusing to see the interests and sincerity of the other. So usually those working somewhere in the middle for reconciliation were seen by both sides as being primarily on the side of the other.

This raises another difficulty for missions. A civil war is so confusing and complex that even missionaries come up with quite differing reports. In good American fashion, that means that one of them has to be lying or covering up. They can't both be sincere. I was reminded of that the day a colleague and I had opportunity to appear before a U.S. congressional study commission led by Rep. Montgomery of Mississippi. The witness ahead of us, a staff member of a large relief agency who happened to be an ex-Marine, gave a glowing report that would have warmed a general's heart. I glanced at Jim Stauffer and asked, "Shall we just save our time and theirs by simply saying that our observations suggest the opposite of everything this person has said?"

Of course, we tried to be more tactful by sharing stories and expressions of feelings from our Vietnamese friends. But we emphasized that the situation is so divided and confused that one can literally make any statement about it and find evidence to prove it. One's own values and priorities determine what one sees or hears.

We urged the congressmen to see the war itself as the only clear indication of how the Vietnamese really think or feel, for the longer it kept grinding on despite incredible odds militarily, the louder the message of their resistance would be to the outside world. The only election in that land that really counted was the one in which men and women, children and grandparents voted with their lives.[4]

Protestants, Catholics, Buddhists, and War

This study has given a rather disparaging picture of Catholic missions in a colonial situation of an earlier era. I need to express a higher regard for the Catholic missions I later observed in the Philippines. The reassessment of the role of the church following Vatican II caused radical shifts. I sense also that they seem now to be using learnings from Vietnam quite effectively in Central America.

One reason for this change, I suggest, is that Catholics in general are now more open and free to look at the issue of war and how missions relate to it. Robert Drinan, the Jesuit politician and former dean of Boston College Law School, made some astute comments regarding this difference already during the Vietnam war.[5] In contrast to the Catholic just war concept, which applies standards and restrictions to warfare, he saw the Protestants tending to hold a crusader position which fosters a holy war mentality. This stance, Drinan says, causes Protestants to be more emotional and less objective in their support of such a cause.

Such comments should challenge Protestant missiologists to give some serious attention to the matter. Certainly in Vietnam, the tendency to see the war as a struggle between the forces of evil (communism) and the forces of good (Western democracy) hindered some missionaries from seeing what was happening around them. Such a holy war view triggers the kind of response given in Victory in Vietnam:

> Two of their church workers had been abducted from a "Christian village" and killed. The two American mission leaders drove out in their Land Rover to check the situation, taking four armed soldiers along. As they drove away following their visit to the village, they looked up at the bravely worded sign in Vietnamese and English.... How desolate the station was now, made so by the atheistic, anti-God, anti-Christ Communists!"[6]

In Vietnam, however, the stark contrast in attitudes toward the war came from Buddhist leaders. The monks were neither united nor faultless in their relationship to the conflict, but their identification with the suffering and the aspirations of their people was truly powerful. Drinan described how astonishing and dramatic it was for him to meet a group of 120 Buddhist monks in one Saigon prison. They declared their imprisonment was for either resisting the draft or advocating peace (which was illegal).

Such a courageous stand spoke forcefully to the people they led, especially since it was undergirded by a handful of leaders who actually offered their lives as a sacrifice for peace. It was nearly impossible for Americans to appreciate the impact of those self-immolations on the Vietnamese—most Americans felt more at home with Madame Nhu's (sister-in-law of President Diem) mockery of them as "human barbecues." Yet I think it would be easier to reconcile self-immolation to Buddha's teaching than a warring spirit to Christ's example.

Back in 1966 I was deeply moved by the words and commitment of a leading monk. He belittled America's talk about fighting to grant them self-determination, when they were but pawns in the hands of world powers. He said they could endure it if the bombing and killing would last only six more months, or even for a year. But he sighed: "There is not one ray of hope. We do not desire communism, but we cannot accept increasingly greater suffering and death for our people."

It would not have solved all problems, but it is fascinating to project what difference it would have made if Christian missions had been as identified with peace and reconciliation as the Buddhists. They were willing to be imprisoned as "traitors" and "peace mongers." But for missions in Vietnam to be seen in the New Testament missionary terms of "peacemakers" and "ambassadors of reconciliation" was purely wishful thinking.

4

The Worldwide Question

*What Was the Impact of Vietnam
on World Missions?*

Fueling the Propaganda Mills

A friend of mine visited Vientiane, Laos, in 1975 following the collapse of U.S. operations in Indochina. He was quite impressed with two pictures drawn in front of the deserted and locked offices of a U.S. Christian relief agency. One picture showed a pastor with a Bible in one hand and a gun in the other. The other drawing portrayed the pastor speaking to a congregation from one side of his mouth and to the CIA from the other side.

Communist propaganda! Sure, it can be shrugged off as that. But is the complicity suggested by the images all that exaggerated? At the least, as the previous chapter suggests, there were elements of reality behind it. And we can be sure that such propaganda has found many receptive audiences across Indochina.

With the majority of the Protestant missionaries having come with, associated with, and left with Uncle Sam and his forces, one can hardly blame the opposition for exploiting the connections and the appearances for their advantage. So again, if we feel comfortable intermingling Christianity with America's self-interests or with an anti-communism religion, there's no need to be concerned. But let us not forget: The Christians left behind in Laos and all Indochina have had to live with those drawings and images.

Earlier I suggested that the war itself was the only meaningful decision-making process available to the people. Others have
made a parallel point regarding the judgment on America's actions. No world tribunal or election will pass sentence on the
USA's disregard of the 1954 international treaties or on its war
conduct. But people across Asia have watched and will remember
for years to come. We will see their vote in that which commands
their respect and commitment.

That tribunal will confront American missions for a generation to come. The image of a powerful, Western, and "Christian"
nation literally raining its fire from the heavens on a mismatched
but heroic ancient people of Asia won't erase easily—no matter
how they feel about communism. It is unfortunate that few
Americans will ever hear the stories of courage, fortitude, and suffering from "the other side" which Asians have been hearing. I
discovered such effects of the war while living in the Philippines
in the '70s, before martial law imposed censorship on the media
there.

Whose Responsibility?

In 1969 a visiting Japanese church leader confirmed my
concerns about the effect of U.S. involvement in Vietnam. He
told how appalled he was at the nationalism of the American missionaries he worked with in Japan—the same persons who threw
up their hands with cries of "nationalism" whenever Japanese believers suggested any changes in the church. He told of repeatedly
observing these missionaries witnessing to Japanese youth, who
would in turn ask about the missionaries' stance on America's actions in Vietnam. After hearing their unquestioning support of the
U.S. policy, the students had no interest in hearing the gospel.

Who is responsible for the fact that vast populations of Asians
have no interest in the Christian message? Why, after many years
of diligent witnessing, do Christians still number less than one
percent in many Asian countries? Christianity is still burdened
with the old colonial images as the religion of the white, wealthy
West. I often agonized over the knowledge that the joint actions

of the U.S. advisers, troops, and missionaries in Vietnam were reinforcing all those repulsive images.

Many mission leaders say that Asia's greatest need is to hear the gospel; they continually appeal for more evangelists, preaching, and media. Isn't it time to give equal attention to another plausible explanation: that the message is being heard and rejected, that Asians don't believe the message because too many negative images stand in their way?

I propose that Christianity's problem in much of the world is that it has an image that repels more than it attracts. To use biblical language, I fear the Asian majorities have already "stopped their ears" and "hardened their hearts"—deciding that if Christianity is what they see and hear, they will have nothing to do with it. It is ironic and embarrassing to read General MacArthur's expectations of how a defeated Japanese people with a devastated ideology would widely embrace the Christian faith following World War II. The 99 percent who have spurned that option should be telling our missions something loud and clear about our image and associations.

A Personal Challenge

I keep hearing the plea of Mr. T_____, a secretary in the premier's office who studied in my English Bible class in Saigon. He was a Buddhist and he had asked how Jesus could be God if he killed and ate fish. The taking of human life was just that much more unthinkable. At the conclusion of the course he wrote:

> "God loved the world so much." But alas!—many churches destroyed, thousands of innocent men dead ... everywhere tears and sighs.... Will God do nothing to relieve this unhappy world? After studying these twelve lessons, I have the idea that the believers—the Christians—must love everyone, whether he is white, black, or yellow; and serve everyone, whether he is a Buddhist, a Christian, or a Muslim. But alas! Since I was a young boy until now, I have seen the followers of Jesus Christ (certainly I don't say all of them) often do very bad things in our country—especially during the war to shake off the yoke of French domination. They have caused much blood to flow. And recently in Saigon you have thousands of Christians with knives in their hands sowing terror in

the streets as they went; and afterward they gathered in a church. What do you think of that? Will they be punished?

I sometimes read the Bible when I was a schoolboy, but I never paid any attention to the words of God. But a new idea came to me when I read your answers on my lesson 4: "... and I could never kill another man, even in self-defense." I must wait until I am 45 to ponder this sentence written by a Christian. And if some- day I still want to be converted, it will depend a great deal on your statement. I think a religion is strong, not by its strength over others, but by its submission and love.

That is the cry of one of Asia's millions trying to believe in a God of love. Mr. T_____ could not hear a religion that is still in- volved in bloodshed and exploitation—from the Crusades of the Middle Ages to Saigon of 1966. Like Mahatma Gandhi of India, he was attracted to Jesus but repelled by his followers.

Anyone truly concerned for evangelism among the religions of·Asia and the Middle East dare not ignore or belittle Chris- tianity's engagement in and association with warfare ever since A.D. 325. "That is the worst stumbling block for missions," con- cluded one church leader who traveled widely in Asia. The Vietnamese were quick to point out that their meditative religions foster peace and brotherhood, while Christianity is an aggressive, militant religion. After all, who fought the world's greatest wars? And who were the oppressive colonial powers? It can all be ra- tionalized, of course, as many a new tribal Christian has belatedly discovered after being convinced to give up his tribal conflicts and vendettas—only to hear the missionary strongly supporting some global conflict against his world neighbors.

These were the burdens churning in my heart that night of the Tet holocaust in Saigon. I became convinced that the greatest witness the church could give on that side of the globe would be a clear denunciation of the associations being encouraged. I knew that the witness would have to be as newsworthy in Asian media as the blessing of the GIs by American evangelists or reports of the president's "praying for God to watch over our boys on their bombing runs each night." Asians were told that God was in- volved in all the destruction and atrocities they saw; but few of them ever heard that any of God's followers objected to the image of those bombs being marked with the Lord's blessing! As far as I know, no missionary was expelled or openly resigned in protest to try to counter that Vietnam connection.[1]

Talking into the Air

Another painful example of missions' indifference to political realities and sensitivities in Asia is the use of radio to go where missionaries are not permitted or desired. As in the use of U-2 planes and spy satellites, missions seem to accomplish their objectives anyway. Maybe that is why there has not been more concern about missions withdrawing from all Indochina. Some seem to feel that evangelism can be done just as well, in fact much easier, by radio.

Complicating the issue of blaring the Christian faith through bamboo curtains is the use of native speakers. Normally this would be excellent; but now those persons are political refugees who have fled. A mission radio agency spent much effort and funds to rescue their Vietnamese staff from Saigon in 1975. These Vietnamese could continue evangelizing their own (or disowned?) people by use of radio in a neighboring country.

I felt frustrated in sharing this concern with the agency. The missionaries simply couldn't see any problem. Let's translate the dynamics closer home. Visualize a disgruntled American youth of the '60s who turned against society, rebelled at the government, escaped to Cuba, and then began to broadcast "the truth" back to his home country. Would we have listened to him? Or worried about his influence? His only audience would have been a few other malcontents like himself, and we would not have cared what he said or did.

I am well aware that these concerns place me in the uncomfortable position of opposing some good and productive mission projects. I have been involved in broadcasting work myself and feel enthusiastic about the great potential of media for missions. But I see it as a medium that must be used with much sensitivity, especially in a transcultural setting.

Again, one can select other priorities and ignore the possibility of doing more harm than good long-range. I plead only for a greater willingness to sit where the masses of Asia sit and to hear through their ears. I plead for the struggling Christian groups who are still so marginal and ineffective in many Asian societies.

Give the Church in Asia a Chance

The following description is typical of many "closing ceremonies" for missionaries throughout South Vietnam in 1975:

> As the "chopper" lifted off and circled above the town, they looked down on the mission house and the Jarai church. When they had arrived ten years before, there was not a believer in the province. They left behind more than a thousand believers—left them in God's presence and care.
>
> It was Tuesday, March 11. A few days later the Communists raised their flag over Cheo Reo.[2]

One does not need to be a communist or even the devil's advocate to realize that both God and that young church were left with a sizable, if not insurmountable, handicap. What were those believers to think as they watched their leader being rescued by the foreign "enemies" in their flying gunships just before the other "enemies"—their fellow citizens—arrived to wave their flag? What could those Christians say when immediately accused as traitors for accepting the religion of the white foreigners? Even worse was the plight of those national pastors or leaders who tried in vain to flee the country with the missionaries and then had to return. They were deserters who must have felt terribly deserted.

No, the Vietnamese Christians were not left simply in God's presence and care; they were left also in a specific world to which they had to relate. They were left, too, with definite attitudes and positions about that new world which suddenly could no longer be ignored. How could the missionaries have left these young churches in a less compromised, stigmatized position? Could we not have prepared them for an easier transition and healthier adjustment to the changes in society about them?[3]

My concern about the consequences of the Vietnam War

was stirred anew by the declaration in 1969 of an American missionary in Japan. He asserted that the Christian mission in Asia is directly dependent on the continued vigorous exercise of Uncle Sam's power. He thereby claimed that the missionaries' interest in evangelizing these nations demanded their support of strong military action as in Vietnam.[4]

The awareness that his position was not typical of all missionaries gave some comfort. Yet I knew many in Vietnam who agreed with that view. And the departure scenes described above suggest that he was right in a self-fulfilling kind of way. How sad if the kingdom of our Lord is so tied to the fortunes and whims of one nation among the billions of people for which God is concerned.

That was back in the Vietnam decade; but the cold war rhetoric and concerns are stirring once more. Now is the time to discuss the problems and to dialogue about the options. Let's ask whose interests and well-being gets priority in determining mission policies and stances. We can't afford to focus only on the immediate crises and preferences with little concern for long-range impacts and wide-reaching images.

5

The Future Question

Will Missions Face Another "Vietnam"?

The Possibility of Similar Conflicts

*R*ecently our newspaper carried an interview article about a local missionary. This person had served in El Salvador for the past twelve years with "an independent, nondenominational missions group." He described the situation there as very critical, fearing economic disaster. The missionary expressed concern about the banks, businesses, and the university—lamenting that "the international businesses have left along with the people with money, land, and professional status." The interview continued: "There is a cancer from Cuba, Nicaragua, and other countries," he says, "the foreigners working among the guerrillas. It is international socialism on the march." He is emphatic that "the U.S. must help or we sink."[1]

The article leaves little doubt where the interests and loyalties of the missionary rest. It makes no reference to the plight of the farmers and workers, and gives no indication as to why socialism is able to march. It only pleads for his superpower back home to intervene and stop it. Interestingly, he reported that their mission is finding good reception among "nominal Catholics" who are disillusioned with their own church because they feel their church leaders have become too involved in politics.

This is just one example from the daily news that points to

51

the likelihood of American missions facing dilemmas similar to the Vietnam situation. If anything, the shift in global dynamics from the old East-West tensions to the newer North-South struggle will likely increase those prospects. In an age of rapidly diminishing resources and unparalleled arms races, the "haves" will be fighting off the desperate "have-nots" no matter what ideology unites them. True, there are masses who already are too malnourished and apathetic to care, but plenty of others see the handwriting on their wall.

If there is any validity in this projected scenario, then our missions will be confronted with increasingly critical issues. Large populations of people to whom we must go with the gospel will be growing in self-awareness and world-consciousness. They will be thinking for themselves, seeing right through the shams we have tended to hide behind in the past. The world of today requires much more humility and honesty than many of us evangelical missionaries have demonstrated since World War II.

Fourteen years of participation in missions among two Asian peoples have led me to conclude that we missionaries have been far too unaware of our impact. One of the affirmations most urgently needed in mission circles is that we can both learn from history and in turn help to shape it. Unfortunately, the record suggests that indeed we have been doing both, except that the influence has been more unconscious than deliberate. Thus, it is often the opposite of God's will and intention that becomes reinforced.

As we shall note later, Jesus was speaking directly to missionaries when he urged: "Be wise as serpents and innocent as doves" (Matthew 10:16). He knew that the challenge of an effective and integral witness calls for astuteness of the highest degree. His own record exhibits such keen analysis and deliberate strategy. He was aware of how his presence and influence was impacting people.

This study suggests that missions would do well to give such dynamics more attention.

What Did We Learn from Vietnam?

Before concluding this review, I readily acknowledge that I have focused on the negative aspects of the Vietnam mission as I perceived them. I have emphasized the ways in which I felt we caused needless offense and avoidable pitfalls. But all this correctly implies that much good work was done in establishing a church with potential for growth.

While many misgivings continue to trouble me about various aspects of that whole experience, I am not arguing that missions should not have been in the midst of the conflict or that I regret having been part of it. In rereading my diaries, letters, and articles from those years, I am impressed anew that Vietnam was a growing, stretching time for us all. Only in later reflection could I point to some specifics in approach, structures, and expectations that would have changed the situation significantly for me.[2]

But why have not all of our missions seen the value of such reflection and assessment? Dare we be content to let bygones be bygones and risk repeating the patterns that have caused so much disruption and hardship for the Christians in China, Cuba, and Vietnam? Why shouldn't we expect each mission involved in such revolutionary upheavals to share an objective analysis of the strengths and weaknesses in its record for the mutual learning and counsel of other missions?

That is precisely what some of us longed for in Saigon during the '60s. We often wondered what the experience in China just twenty years earlier would suggest we do in preparation for the possibility of a similar outcome.[3] We read all we could, but the brief sketches we had available were not all that helpful. And the largely negative China stories that floated around only aroused more apprehension, reinforcing lessons that tended simply to repeat the experience.

Imagine what a resource it would have been to have a composite picture of that transition drawn from the many missions and strategies across the regions of China. From the general forms of accusations and adjustments with which the Christians were confronted, missiologists could have outlined positions and strategies to reduce the fallout and strengthen the local character of the church. Of course, such a resource would require as much research and writing as has been devoted to the subject of church growth in recent decades, but it appears that missions are fascinated by the more spectacular growth settings.

Instead, our nearly automatic reactions in 1975 were evidence that missions had learned something in China. We knew that the communists would kick out all foreign missionaries—not recognizing that French priests still served in North Vietnam—and would openly attack the church. So I suggest the question is not whether we learned from China, but what we learned and how. Was it blind reinforcement or improvement of performance? The distinction is vital for missions on the threshold of the twenty-first century.

This is a call for us as loyal subjects of the Lord of history to take more credit and responsibility for the shaping of history: past, present, and future. Surely we can acknowledge some cause-and-effect relationships behind the closed doors and the rejecting majorities that confront Christian missions in Asia.

Such self-critical measures and corrections will not always change or even alter the course of history. But they will create much greater flexibility and adaptability by missions at every twist and turn, enhancing the influence of God's witness on the stream of events.

SHALOM IS GOD'S MISSION

6

The Vision

Upholding the Good Life

*T*he Bible is the account of a mission. It records the mission of a loving God who would not give up that mission despite many setbacks. The mission, begun in Genesis, will conclude triumphantly in the scenes of Revelation, and will encompass our mission today insofar as we are participating in God's program of the 1980s.

There are many ways to perceive and describe this divine mission. One of those ways is through shalom, a term that has been associated with God's cause from beginning to end. It says a great deal about the message and the means, the purpose and the goal of the Lord's mission in the world.

Shalom offers specific guidelines for the issues and dilemmas raised by the Vietnam sojourn. This study has grown out of my experience of confusion and frustration in that encounter. It reflects my search for and reconstruction of a relevant, effective mission in such a chaotic and troubled world.

The Truly Good Life
We looked for *shalom*, but no good came,
for a time of healing, but behold, terror
Jeremiah 8:15; 14:19.

Shalom is a difficult concept to grasp because it describes a quality of life that defies a one-word translation. The word is recognized universally as the traditional Jewish greeting and fare-well—from Abraham's day to the present. At the same time it is one of the most comprehensive theological terms in the Scrip-tures. Walter Brueggemann writes that the term "bears tremen-dous freight, the freight of a dream of God that resists all our tendencies to division, hostility, fear, drivenness, and misery."[1]

Words always reflect the perceptions of the people using them. Sometimes in the same setting a speaker and a listener can give the same word different meanings. Since shalom was used so broadly in history and cultures, our understanding of it is espe-cially dependent on our knowledge of the life and thought of the people using it. Thus we are indebted to modern scholarship on ancient Israel for the renewed interest in the usage of the term.

But we encounter a translation problem because the use of shalom was so varied that its precise meaning in any verse must often be derived from the context. As one Hebrew scholar put it, "There is something imprecise about it in almost every instance."[2] Our English Bible also seems to limit the word's impact by simply using "peace" in most places. That is what shalom usually does not mean, since we tend to think in terms of the Greek (eirēnē) or Latin (pax) meanings.[3]

The problem is compounded in the New Testament, since the Greek text naturally uses the term eirēnē. But what is the rela-tionship between the Old Testament shalom and the New Testa-ment eirēnē? While the predominent use of eirēnē in the Greek world referred to political stability and order (i.e., the absence of war which was viewed as the natural state), eirēnē in the New Testament reflects deep roots in the Hebrew shalom. Repeatedly we find the same images and associations which tie eirēnē to God's vision of the truly good life.[4]

One way to get quickly into the biblical framework is to do some dreaming. To begin thinking in the aura and spirit of shalom, pause and draw a mental picture of life at its best, life as good as we can imagine it to be. Note the settings that emerge and the feelings that begin to stir.

That's it! That is the stuff of which shalom is made. It relates to our desires and longings. The fact that we can conceive of a beautiful life, however utopian, says something about its possibility and our potential. Just to project the "spirit of Christmas" for the other 364 days a year would be a wonderful change in the world. Allowing our imagination to run wildly does something to our spirits. We all know we could experience more goodness in life if we really wanted to. That's the excitement of shalom—meeting us right where we are and stirring new hope to reach higher.

The Original Dream

The exercise we just did parallels the way the biblical story begins. Genesis 1 and 2 is God's portrait of the good life as the biblical authors conceived it. Our dreams of the good life usually stay quite close to the original paradise. Even though the Garden of Eden may seem quite foreign to our present life, somehow it feels natural and instinctively right. Dreams of the good life are like longings of home. They create an awareness that we are missing something that we were meant to enjoy.

That something is shalom. It is God's vision for the created world. It is life as it was intended to be according to the original design. Instead of trying to describe it for us, the Spirit inspired the writers to paint a picture of shalom in the story of Eden. They portrayed the primeval setting in a way that envisioned for all time what life truly can be.

The meaning and purpose of the vision is not explicit in the Genesis account. Shalom is not even mentioned in those opening chapters. But we shall note later that at the time of the prophets, when the story of Eden was used effectively for God's people, the shalom dynamic was so obvious that it did not need to be spelled out. They were desperately looking for a vision of life as the Creator wanted it to be.

The concept of shalom centers on the web of relationships between all the parts of creation. Shalom reigned so long as each part fulfilled its purpose in a mutually beneficial way for every other part to do the same. The result of such harmonious interaction and fulfillment is incredible paradise. While redemption and restoration bring new dimensions to counter the anti-shalom of the fall, this picture of the truly good life cannot be improved.

Themes from Creation

The exhilarating atmosphere around the idea of creation ties directly to the energy of shalom. They both point to the fact that things do not remain the same. We are not chained to the past. The possibility of starting over, the power to make new, and the prospect of another day keep hope alive. The Bible shows this hope as rooted in the nature of the Creator. God's call to Israel was:

> Behold, I am doing a new thing;
>> now it springs forth, do you not perceive it?
>>> *Isaiah 43:19.*

Even the idea of an entirely "new heaven and new earth" is an intriguing concept for both Testaments (Isaiah 65:17; 66:22; 2 Peter 3:13; Revelation 21:1), closing with the quotation from the throne: "Behold, I make all things new" (Revelation 21:5).

The theme of newness was surely a vital aspect of the original shalom scene. Eden's shalom was perfect because everything was just the way God made it—connecting the possibility of shalom directly to the creative powers of God. Out of the primeval chaos, void, and darkness the Creator had planned and formed an orderly and purposeful world. And that sparkling new world radiated unmarred—though untested—shalom.

The Creator looked over that work with complete satisfaction: "Behold, it was very good" (Genesis 1:31). Shalom affirms that the truly good life is the natural state for all creation, and that all creation is truly good, with a place and purpose for every part. That includes the limitations inherent in a created world.

In that "very good" world was the testing tree and the power of choice it symbolized. We cannot tell how long Adam and Eve exercised this power with a positive response. (Did the shalom last for days, years, or ages?) But we know that the potential of breaking relationship through envy and rebellion was part of the original and purposeful good. Even in Eden there would have been no shalom without opportunity for response, and it lasted as long as the people chose to be faithful. They were response-able.

Notice the test. It was not based directly on beliefs, morals, or ethics, but on the physical world. Our spirituality is connected to the fruit of the earth; our shalom is tied to the world about us. The shalom of all creation depended on the man and woman using their godlike powers of choice to express their accountability in their use of the material world.

The shalom of Eden also pointed to the need for community and companionship. "It is not good that the man should be alone" (Genesis 2:18) indicates that shalom requires a caring relationship. Our visions usually suggest the fewer the people, the greater the chance for peace and happiness. But the order to "multiply and fill the earth" was part of the original vision. Shalom affirms that the broader the community, the greater the potential for prosperity and security for all. Each is dependent on what the others supply. So the vision moves toward a city.

The Divine Mission

God created the world to live in shalom. But the fall broke relationships and ended harmony. The various parts could no longer interact or function properly with the sense of balance and trust that they knew before. The spirit of mutuality was fractured into small private worlds—each creature on its own watching out for itself.

A spirit of alienation became the main characteristic, even separating Yahweh from the creation. No longer did God enjoy communion with this world, as pictured in the daily "walking in the garden in the cool of the day" (Genesis 3:8). God had allowed the man and woman to cut off their relationship of trust and faithfulness by an act of defiance against their limitations. Now they all suffered the consequences of that power.

But the new situation gave the Creator a chance to say, "Shalom." If shalom is life as God made it, then shalom is life as God still intended it to be. Yahweh embarked on a grand mission, stretching across the ages to restore that original vision. The New

Testament writers pictured God as being involved in mission since "the foundation of the world" (Ephesians 1:4; 1 Peter 1:20; Revelation 13:8). The dominant theme of that salvation mission is that God is overcoming the estrangement caused by the fall.

Hence the motif "Paradise Lost—Paradise Regained" is a fitting caption for the cause in which the Creator-Redeemer has been engaged ever since. Yahweh has been portrayed as a caring and tireless shepherd (Psalm 23, Ezekiel 34, John 10), never allowing people to forget the life they were meant to enjoy. The vision of Eden's shalom continued through the centuries—haunting, prodding, and teasing persons to keep stretching toward that dream. It has often seemed like an impossible dream, but an instinctive, tormenting restlessness will not let it die.

The Scriptures also portray God with a parallel restless desire to live with a responsive people again. Yahweh has patiently sought out a special people for interaction and relationship. The prophets spoke of this yearning in the warm endearing terms of marriage and sexual love. Repeatedly they associated this longing to live and rule among God's people with the shalom vision.

This brings us to the political aspect of shalom. The biblical concept sees power and politics as key elements of shalom and specific concerns of mission. In fact, the divine mission as pictured in the Bible probably has more to do with politics than any other aspect of human life. One definition of politics is the total web of relationships between persons in a society, which closely parallels the context of shalom.

God relates to humans as their maker and ruler. The divine message proclaims: "He is Lord of all" (Acts 10:36). The name is "King of kings and Lord of lords" (Revelation 19:16). So any positive response to such claims in life immediately calls into question all other allegiances and power. That is why the most dominant theme in Jesus' preaching was the kingdom (rule) of God.

The New Creation
Mission refers to what this Lord is about in the world. It relates to the design, operation, and objective of God's work in

bringing restoration to creation. The loving concern of a gracious Lord will not allow a ruined world to be forgotten or wiped out. God embarked on a mission to reestablish relations on earth.

The Bible speaks of this mission being accomplished again by God's creative power, this time to restore and renew the fallen. Jeremiah foresaw that "the Lord has created a new thing on the earth" (31:22). Paul believed this was fulfilled in the work of Christ which he called "a new creation" (2 Corinthians 5:17). He also spoke of "the new nature, which is being renewed in knowledge after the image of its creator" (Colossians 3:10). What a powerful and intoxicating concept of God's work in the new covenant! "Power" is a favorite term for Paul to describe God's mission at work (Romans 1:16; 1 Corinthians 1:18; 4:20).

But no word captures the life-giving, exuberant character of the divine mission as does the term shalom. Again and again, God is "the God of shalom" (Philippians 4:9), the message is "the gospel of shalom" (Ephesians 6:15), and the agent-son "is shalom" (Ephesians 2:14) personified. One cannot help but get caught up in the excitement and joy of the prophets who dreamed of the new "covenant of shalom" (Ezekiel 34:25) and of the early church who saw themselves experiencing it. This is the mission of a loving God who kept offering shalom to an alienated people.

The inspired visions of John anticipated a successful mission—that God will accomplish what he is about. The closing scene (Revelation 21:1—22:5) is strikingly parallel to the opening scene in Genesis. Once again there is a garden with a river, abundant fruit and leaves, and the tree of life. Only now the garden is in the middle of a city with open gates and streets. God's mission has caused Adam and Eve to become "the nations." Yet the same spirit of harmony, wholeness, and community surrounds it all. And God is there with all those who responded.

In this brief passage John mentions twenty-five anti-shalom items that will be no more, because "the former things have passed away" (Revelation 21:4). There will be no more death, sea, night, mourning, pain, temple, immorality, dishonesty, doubt. "Behold, I make all things new" (v. 5) is God's announcement of restored shalom. It includes radiant light, glory, beauty, worship, symbols of life and healing, of kingship and honor, of family and community. God and the people are enjoying shalom in a brand-new world.

A list of themes used in connection with shalom may be helpful to give a fuller idea of its meaning and effect. Many of these words are used in parallel associations with shalom, suggesting an overlapping or similar meaning. The order reflects somewhat the development in biblical history from the material and social to more theological concepts. The ideas are sharpened with a corresponding list of contrasts, as the Bible often does.[4] The list is neither complete nor perfect, but it should aid in our awareness, reflection, and study.

Shalom *(what God wills)*	*Anti-shalom* *(what God opposes)*
1. Wholeness and strength	Brokenness and brittleness
2. Well-being and prosperity	Misery and adversity
3. Blessing and good will	Curses and ill-will
4. Health and happiness	Illness and sadness
5. Security and safety	Anxiety and peril
6. Identity and solidarity	Lostness and alienation
7. Freedom and response	Oppression and coercion
8. Power and action	Impotence and frustration
9. Reconciliation and restoration	Enmity and discord
10. Acceptance and love	Rejection and hostility
11. Care and community	Indifference and selfishness
12. Harmony and mutuality	Strife and inequality
13. Commitment and faithfulness	Instability and disloyalty
14. Justice and righteousness	Partiality and corruption
15. Order and purpose	Chaos and confusion
16. Celebration and hope	Desperation and futility
17. Completion and perfection	Failure and ruin
18. Salvation and life	Damnation and death

o o o

Shalom is the courage to be . . .
all that the Lord wants me to be . . .
living out a vision that only God can make real.

7

The Community

Creating Peoplehood Through Covenant

Once you were not a people,
but now you are the people of God.
1 Peter 2:10, NIV.

Identity and Belonging

*T*he earliest usage of shalom is in the context of kinship and tribal relations. The word seems to denote a sense of identification, solidarity, and security within the family or clan. It describes the feeling of belonging and of commonality with the tribe—the sense of peoplehood. The need for that awareness was strong. The bond of shalom had to be real enough to be seen and felt. It was the glue that held life in place.[1]

Since any arrival or departure affected the well-being of the group in an organic way, concern for shalom was expressed at those times. A newcomer had to pledge to uphold the shalom of the group. Thus Samuel was asked by David's village, "Do you come in *shalom*?" (1 Samuel 16:4, NIV)—seeking a declaration of having no intention to disrupt the harmony of the clan.

Departure required the same commitment. To part in shalom assured the group that the separation would not be an occasion for any ill will or revenge behind their backs. So Moses and his father-in-law parted and met again with the pledge for each other's well-being (Exodus 4:18; 18:7). Such usage gives an obvious sense of blessing and fidelity, creating an early connotation of desirable goodness and security (salvation).[2]

Conversely, there must have been an awareness that whatever destroyed the welfare of the tribe was undesirable and evil. This can be seen during the troubled times in Jacob's household between Joseph and his brothers. Barriers of time and space disturbed shalom (Genesis 37:14; 43:27, 28), but it could be devastated in the emotional distance caused by jealousy right within the tent (37:4). Yet Joseph testified that with Yahweh's help even an intention of evil, which Reuben called "sin" (42:22), could be turned into good (50:20). From early times God was viewed as having power to create shalom out of a destructive situation.

Stories of the patriarchs reveal the ability to bless and to curse to be an awesome power. The life-and-death struggle between Jacob and Esau is a good example (Genesis 27; see also chapter 49). But Yahweh held ultimate power in blessing (12:2, 3) and cursing (3:14ff.). Increasingly shalom came to be associated with God and the blessing which heaven could bestow or withhold. The call was for persons to participate in the divine mission as a channel of shalom:

> . . . all peoples on earth will be blessed through you (12:3, NIV).

From Kinship to Covenant

The call of Abraham demonstrated that a shalom relationship could be created where none existed. As civilization developed, it became desirable to extend the bonds of shalom beyond natural ties. Unrelated persons or groups could have the same desire to seek each other's good—and pledge themselves to do it. So the same sense of peoplehood was created by making agreements or treaties.

This could be done even when trouble arose and shalom was shattered. The option of restoring harmony by making a covenant, rather than beginning a cycle of vengeance or a battle-to-the-end, was increasingly appealing. So we see Isaac and

Abimelech settling their dispute by promising to do "no harm . . . nothing but good" (Genesis 26:26-33; see also 21:22-32). They sealed the treaty with the usual covenant meal and parted "in *shalom.*" These patriarchal examples of shalom-making were shining models.

In his writing on Hebrew life and thought, still viewed as a foundational study today, Pedersen stressed that the Hebrews perceived shalom as the essence of reality.[3] Shalom referred to "souls-in-community" who could function and grow *only* in conjunction with other souls. It meant having a common will and responsibility; to live in "one will" relationships. Pedersen claimed that the Hebrews did not distinguish between love and shalom, since both refer to having identical wills. Hence to live in shalom means the same thing as loving your neighbor as yourself (Leviticus 19:18, 34); it means to desire good for one another.

Life for the Hebrew was unthinkable apart from the promise of shalom pledged by covenants. Remove the covenants, and the world would literally fall apart. A beautiful example of what could be done through covenant is seen in the commitment of Jonathan to save David's life from his father's jealousy (1 Samuel 18:3; 20:8, 42; 23:18). Their shalom relationship was so close that "he loved him as he loved his own soul" (20:17).

Yahweh Is a Covenanting God

That God should choose treaty-making as the way to establish and maintain relationships with his people is highly significant. It provides a basis for Yahweh's action to enable the fallen human race to regain a sense of Eden. The covenant concept says a great deal about both God and the chosen people, as well as the nature of their association. Charles West points out this uniqueness well:

> In biblical history, peace is the result of a covenant in which the two parties accept and affirm each other in a relationship which is open-ended and in which both will themselves be changed. It is through this quite secular and humanly dynamic channel that YHWH chose to reveal himself and establish his rela-

tion to his people. Covenant peace is therefore not immutable rest, but the moving drama of human interaction and self-realization informed and reformed by God.[4]

The idea of this living, ever-changing, growing relationship between God and those who respond to the divine call is illustrated well in the life of Abraham. The summary in Hebrews ("By faith he sojourned in the land of promise"—11:9) captures this focus on the relational. Living with Yahweh meant a walk of faith; it meant living as pilgrims on earth (11:13-16). The nature of faith itself suggested that shalom is based on a living covenant-agreement with God. This stands in contrast to the more permanent, fixed type of institutions of other peoples, such as codes, temples, empires, and dynasties.[5]

The covenant began in Egypt when Yahweh heard the Israelites' cry and recognized their sufferings (Exodus 3:7-9). God "remembered [the] covenant" made with Abraham, Isaac, and Jacob (6:4, 5). The mission of the Almighty took new shape in sending Moses who had already been prepared for the task. But when the slaves were told of Yahweh's promised deliverance, "they did not listen to Moses, because of their broken spirit and their cruel bondage" (6:9).

This situation pinpoints two basic ingredients of shalom that are essential also to missions: freedom and response. True shalom cannot exist apart from a voluntary response and firm commitment to it by the persons involved. Shalom is possible only to those who desire it and work for it. God has taken the initiative to make it possible, giving the vision for it and offering it to every person. Yet that does not make shalom.

A free and spontaneous response is required for covenanting. It takes two parties to make a covenant. If there is no mutuality in the process, the one simply is submitting to the superiority and obeying the demands of the other. Since a covenant's effectiveness in keeping shalom depends on how carefully it is observed, the extent of mutual ownership from the start determines its success.

The two parties do not need to be equals, else we would have no chance with God. The Israelites were told to "offer terms of *shalom*" before attacking cities (Deuteronomy 20:10ff.), an option which Jesus also suggested for a threatened group (Luke 14:32). Both passages indicate that those terms of shalom can be accepted or rejected—with consequences, of course. But no one can be forced to enter into a covenant relationship. As in marriage, a covenant lasts only so long as both parties embrace it freely—without force—and fully—without reservation.

That points to the other ingredient: freedom. Shalom is not for slaves. How can one who is enslaved choose other options or take action to change anything? The ability to act decisively is the twin requirement to the voluntary response needed for a covenant. This free commitment of one's devotion, energy, and resources creates the power which God uses in the world. As people band together in common cause, they can create enough political power to move mountains and change the minds of kings.

The matter of false shalom will be addressed later, but it needs to be recognized here, since slaves do develop a deceptive sense of shalom (security). Coercion and oppression must be seen as the adversaries of real shalom, for they crush the spirit and make it impossible to choose, act, and grow. That was what Moses found in Egypt. How shocking it must have been for him to learn the second time that slaves don't always want freedom (Exodus 2:14; 6:9)!

For people accustomed to bondage, freedom can be a terrifying risk. Jesus' question, "Do you want to be healed?" (John 5:6) still needs to be asked today of people in anti-shalom conditions. It requires such faith to venture into the unknown, such courage for taking risks, such responsibility to accept commitments that many people cannot respond. Both the Israelites (Exodus 16:3; Numbers 14:2-4) and the Galatians (Galatians 3:1; 4:8, 9; 5:1) looked back to the comfort of the old chains. To enter into covenant with God is the toughest challenge anyone can accept.

> No one who puts his hand to the plow and looks back is fit for service in the kingdom of God.
>
> *Luke 9:62, NIV.*

Forming a Covenant People

God comes to men and women with clear terms of shalom. Abraham was told, "I am God Almighty; walk before me, and be blameless. And I will make my covenant between me and you" (Genesis 17:1, 2). The covenant later took the form of the Decalogue, prefaced with the reminder that Yahweh's power in their deliverance made this covenant a possibility. The Law given on the Mount, called "the book of the covenant" (Exodus 24:7), established the treaty conditions in great detail. The people responded, "All that the Lord has spoken we will do," and they celebrated the covenant with a meal in God's presence (7, 11).

The teaching of the prophets developed the covenant requirements in ever sharper ethical terms. They insisted repeatedly that to speak of shalom without justice and righteousness in every dimension of society was a contradiction in terms. Psalm 85 shows how shalom-salvation was linked directly to faithfulness and right living in daily life. The prophets continually reminded the people of Yahweh that they were bound in covenant to live by God's order.

Yet people were aware that something more was needed. A popular oracle envisioned the people beating their swords and spears into tools of production. But such radical conversion required a living example of God's will:

> Come, let us go up to the mountain of the Lord,
>   to the house of the God of Jacob;
> that he may teach us his ways
>   and that we may walk in his paths."
>
> Isaiah 2:3; Micah 4:2.

So in time Messiah came with a "much more excellent" ministry and covenant (Hebrews 8:6). But the relationship and appeal did not change. God was still calling out a people who would commit themselves to this vision. Jesus announced God's will for all people from the Mount, with even higher standards focusing on inner motives, attitudes, and values (Matthew 5—7). However, this time the mediator of the covenant was able to show in his own life that the conditions could be met. The New Testament affirms that God came and lived among us to communicate clearly by example and teaching the shalom-life intended for us. As Jesus put it:

> If I had not come and spoken to them, they would not have sin; but now they have no excuse for their sin.
> *John 15:22.*

No excuse for sin! The New Testament writers continued in the same pattern as the prophets in spelling out God's expectations of covenant. Only now the application needed to be transcultural and universal. We see again that the meanings of shalom can never be fixed once for all, but must relate integrally to all persons and their settings. Yet the appeals sound familiar, as we note in this sample from Paul:

> Aim for perfection, listen to my appeal, be of one mind, live in *shalom*. And the God of love and *shalom* will be with you.
> *2 Corinthians 13:11, NIV.*

Paul here associates shalom with themes we have noted before: perfection, mutual address, commonality, and God's presence. The divine mission still is pressing for the same vision.

Dealing with Broken Vows

As we often see in biblical history, covenants are more easily made than kept. Since one is free to enter into an agreement, one is also free to go against this pledge and break it. This is the relational nature of shalom, requiring continual renewal and steadfast faithfulness. Hence, both society and God have needed to find and regulate the ways and means of restoring harmony after failure.

The ancient Hebrew word *shillem* (to make a payment of compensation to correct a wrong) comes from the same root word as shalom. Something must be done to make up for the hurt or offense resulting from the broken shalom, so that the situation is restored to balance and wholeness. Blood vengeance between tribes was an early form of this concept. Some of the world's most ancient laws such as the *lex talionis* sought to regulate this balancing effort.[6]

This concept was soon given religious significance with meals, offerings, and sacrifices. Ancient societies, after offering food to the tribal gods, ate sacrificial meals together to strengthen the bonds of community and sense of harmony. This was especially needed after storms, drought, disease, and war had stirred feelings of anxiety and alienation.

The complex sacrificial system instituted in the Mosaic covenant can be similarly understood. Hugh White writes about the sacrificial meal known as the peace offering *(shelamin)* in this way:

> [It] refers simply to the restoration of community with God. Since a victim is sacrificed, this reconciliation with God stems from a *shillem*, a repayment. The peace offering is thus both a sacrament restoring lost unity, and a gift in compensation for acts of transgression. The feeling of having offended God is in some way expressed and absolved through this kind of compensatory act.[7]

So God made provision for restitution and restoration when sin had broken the covenant and disrupted shalom. Showing great patience and mercy, the Lord was always ready to start over anew as long as the people admitted their unfaithfulness and returned to fidelity. The drama of Hosea and the love stories of Ezekiel reveal the intensity of Yahweh's yearning to have a responsive people who would love wholeheartedly in return.

The Levitical sacrifices prescribed the ritual for dealing with estrangement following unfaithfulness, but the system could produce little motivational or life-changing power. The prophets certainly realized this. They knew that "thousands of rams," or "ten thousand rivers of oil," or even offering "my firstborn ... the fruit of my body for the sin of my soul" could never replace doing justice, loving kindness, and walking humbly with God (Micah 6:6-8, NIV). But how could one attain such faithfulness?

In the shalom passages of Isaiah the prophets began to dream of one who suffers vicariously for the sins of others (Isaiah 53). Like a sheep offered as sacrifice in the place of the guilty person, this innocent one would offer to take the sinner's place. The suffering servant would stop both the endless cycle of revenge and rebellion as well as the indifference of countless ritual sacrifices. The body of this servant would absorb all the hostility. Such suffering love would bring healing and wholeness, the basis of a new community.

That need reflected great insight into the nature of shalom and the miserable failings of humanity. It is no surprise that John opened his story of the Messiah's work with the Baptist's cry:

> Behold, the Lamb of God, who takes away the sin of the world! (1:29).

The New Testament writers viewed the life and death of Jesus as fulfilling that role of the suffering servant. Jesus' own testimony was that he came "to serve, and to give his life as a ransom for many" (Mark 10:45).

Christ not only removed our excuses by showing the ways of God most clearly; he also provided the means for every person to follow that way. The new covenant was based on a dramatic act of deliverance and freedom just as the old one was. The cross became the new symbol of exodus, and the Lord's supper became the new covenant meal. The power of the resurrection now available to work in us is a greater power than Egypt ever saw.

So the possibility of shalom—in the New Testament, *eirēnē*—is now open to every person, regardless of race, sex, or status. Jews and Greeks, slaves and free, men and women all become "one will" in Jesus Christ (Galatians 3:28). Jesus said that through the cross he would draw all peoples to God (John 12:32). Immediately before and after that covenant-making event, Christ identified his ministry with shalom (John 14:27; 16:33; 20:21, 26). In Luke Jesus announced the gospel as a call to shalom (4:18ff.), the *eirēnē*-peace of the kingdom. The basis of this shalom is the power of self-giving love as the sacrificial lamb of God.

Paul's insight in Ephesians 2 explicitly shows how the cross created the new shalom community. The death of Christ breaks down social barriers and absorbs the hostilities which people have for each other. All people who respond are brought together into a new community without walls or ranks. Jesus made shalom a reality by creating a new humanity, joining God's people in a common life in a single household.

No wonder Paul used Micah's vision (Micah 5:5) to exclaim, "He is our *shalom!*" He described the ministry of Jesus as simply proclaiming shalom to both Jews and Gentiles (Ephesians 2:14, 17, NIV). The alienation caused by the fall was overcome as all people came together in Christ. God's mission now became truly universal, for the definition of Christ's shalom requires that people of differing races and backgrounds be able to commune together. At last the lion and the lamb could live in harmony and security as both the Roman and the Jew discovered that they were equally loved and lovable.

o o o

Shalom is the freedom to become ...
the people God meant for us to be ...
covenanted together in the common life of the Spirit.

8

The Power

Living with God as King

> Your kingdom come,
> Your will be done
>   on earth as it is in heaven.
> *Matthew 6:10, NIV.*

*H*ow glibly we often say these parallel phrases in which Jesus taught his followers to commit themselves to help fulfill his mission on earth. Capturing the vision of the good life depends on God's rule being accepted and God's will being done. We can have no greater purpose or nobler aspiration. The closer we come to fulfilling this mission-prayer, the greater shalom we shall enjoy.

"The Lord Your God Was Your King"

This terse statement in 1 Samuel 12:12 describes God's relationship to Israel from the exodus through the judges. The Israelites were a special people because Yahweh was their ruler, leading and saving those who trustingly submitted to that rule. They had been chosen and set free for that purpose:

> I am the Lord, and I will bring you out . . . I will deliver you from their bondage, and I will redeem you . . . and I will take you for my people, and I will be your God.
> *Exodus 6:6, 7.*

The covenant law taught Israel how to order its life accord-

75

ing to the new king's design. Since chaos and confusion work against shalom, the Lord spelled out this order for all aspects of life. The covenant contained repeated appeals for obedience and loyalty to this rule, which would result in the blessings of shalom.

That must have been an exhilarating time as those former slaves learned to be a nation under God. Although we tend to focus on the times of grumbling, faithlessness, and rebellion, the prophets later described this as the honeymoon time for Yahweh and Israel, when their love and devotion was most warm and tender. Their relationship was symbolized by the tabernacle as the place of God's presence among the people. This was dramatized day and night in the pillar of cloud and fire, moving or resting to express the will of their King (see Exodus 13:21ff.; Numbers 9:15ff.).

Worship was a political ceremony. The people gave to the Lord the allegiance and homage (honor and glory) that every king demands.[1] They were a pilgrim people, wholly dependent on their ruler for daily direction, sustenance, and deliverance. The manna was a daily reminder that their shalom was a gift from Yahweh.

This was the framework for Israel to understand national security as well. The threat of an enemy force was not a test of military strength or skill, for the outcome did not depend on numbers, training, or strategy. Warfare tested their faith and allegiance to Yahweh, whose victory was seen as salvation (Exodus 14:13; 15:2).[2] The triumph over Egypt was the pattern whereby Israel was to accept the fact that its existence depended on God's holy war on its behalf.

Such keen awareness of Israel's need and God's care must have fostered a sense of intimate trust. Though we read little of its theological importance in the narrative, this time was viewed as a happy, satisfying experience:

> I remember the devotion of your youth,
>   your love as a bride,
> how you followed me in the wilderness.
>
> *Jeremiah 2:2.*

In fact, Hosea quotes God as wanting to bring Israel back "into the wilderness, and speak tenderly to her. . . . And there she shall answer as in the days of her youth" (Hosea 2:14, 15).

Becoming Like All the Nations

As Ezekiel's love story vividly portrayed, the honeymoon did not last: "You became very beautiful and rose to be a queen" (Ezekiel 16:13, NIV). Israel's determination to have a king with all the trappings of royalty and empire was a radical setback to the divine mission. Yahweh perceived it as rejecting "me from being king over them," but went along with their adulterous desire to be like others (1 Samuel 8:7). Israel could not be as all the other nations (v. 5) and still be special. God's angry reaction was expressed most bluntly in Hosea's allegory:

> Every evil of theirs is in Gilgal; there I began to hate them ... I will drive them out of my house. I will love them no more (9:15).[3]

As Samuel predicted, tensions arose quickly. Increasingly the earthly king's desires and actions determined the common will and responsibility. Israel's shalom soon was secured by permanent institutions: thrones, dynasties, and temple. This called for a state religion with its own school of prophets to assure control.

Now security came from alliances which included official intermarriages, requiring palaces and harems. A standing, trained militia put Israel's warfare on the same level as other nations. It could enforce the will and whim of the king, resulting in a law-and-order shalom. It was a major move backwards, and all kinds of intrigue, injustice, and oppression followed.[4]

The stage was set for sharp conflict between the prophets supporting the empire and the prophets whom God called as special messengers. Both claimed to represent Yahweh and the concern for order.[5] The issue was if shalom required faithfulness to the covenant and righteous living, or could it be based on the king's power to provide security and stability.

Both could not be right. So we have a new term: false

shalom. Repeatedly the prophets of God mocked the assurances of the professionals: " '*Shalom, shalom,*' they say, when there is no *shalom*" (Jeremiah 6:14, NIV). Ezekiel's blistering words against the delusive visions, lying revelations, and misleading hopes of the king's prophets show how severe and complex the controversy had become (Ezekiel 13). Jeremiah even complained to Yahweh that they were promising "assured *shalom* (eternal salvation) in this place" in God's name (Jeremiah 14:13). Later Jeremiah came back with this word from God:

> I have taken away my *shalom* from this people.... For behold, every one of you follows his stubborn evil will (16:5, 12).

We can call those court prophets false because we know now they were not speaking God's views. But it seems more accurate to speak of a true and false shalom, with each viewpoint having sincere followers. Both could make a rational case, since Israel appeared fairly strong on the surface. The fact that many Christians view the earlier years of the kingdom as Israel's Golden Age indicates how badly we have misunderstood God's mission. Yahweh's prophets called it adultery.

Judgment and Hope

The fall of Jerusalem dealt a deathblow to the aspiration that state and cult could replace obedience to God and the covenant as the foundation of shalom. The people had put their faith in the assurance of Jerusalem as God's eternal dwelling place and in David's everlasting throne (Jeremiah 7). John Bright says it well:

> Nebuchadnezzar's battering rams of course breached that theology beyond repair. It was a false theology, and the prophets who had proclaimed it had lied.
> *Lamentations 2:14.*[6]

Their shalom based on empire, throne, temple, and sword had to be forever shattered. Yahweh's messengers paid dearly for their open opposition to that false vision and oppressive power, as Jesus recognized (Matthew 23:29-39). But in the end, the ability of the remnant to refocus faith was a marvel credited to faithful witnesses of Yahweh's mission.

Out of those ruins of false hopes came opportunity to see new visions. The treaty between God and the people would be restored; the mission would get back on track once more. Ezekiel pictured Yahweh forsaking the temple, throne, and city (chapters 10, 11), but not the people. God would go with them in exile and bring them back. They were to accept this judgment on their apostasy and make the best of their exile:

> I know the plans I have for you, says the Lord, plans for *shalom* . . . to give you a future and a hope.
>
> *Jeremiah 29:11.*

That hope stirred the wildest dreams of the prophets. They envisioned a brand-new covenant, "a covenant of *shalom*" (Ezekiel 34:25; 37:26), that would restore things as they were in Eden. The prophets looked back to the original and projected the same spirit of harmony and wholeness for all creation in this future covenant (Ezekiel 36:35; Isaiah 51:3; 11:1-9). Nearly all descriptions of the messianic age were remarkably like the Eden setting. They anticipated "paradise regained."

One major difference in the new age would be a radical transformation within each person who covenants with the Lord. Tender hearts and responsive spirits would enable people to follow their God (Ezekiel 36:26, 27; Jeremiah 31:33). But the picture repeated most often is that of God again living among these people as ruler:

> I will make a covenant of *shalom* with them . . . and will set my sanctuary in the midst of them for evermore. My dwelling place shall be with them; and I will be their God, and they shall be my people. . . . And they shall know that I, the Lord their God, am with them, and that they, the house of Israel, are my people, says the Lord God.
>
> *Ezekiel 37:26, 27; 34:30.*

Jesus and the Kingdom

This set the stage for Jesus to usher in the new covenant by announcing that the awaited rule of God was now beginning.[7]

Jesus' ministry is described as having a dual thrust: (1) healing the sick and (2) preaching the kingdom of God (Matthew 4:23; 9:35; Luke 9:11). This proclamation of God's reign brought with it a call for repentance, a radical turning-around response. One could not hear this good news without an about-face in life. The appeal was, "Come, follow me," calling for the same full response and total allegiance as the old covenant.

Shalom helps us to see that God's rule is the reality behind the new covenant. The divine mission was in full operation. Jesus' claim that God was ruling on earth once again was the sign for the age of shalom. Dormant hopes and expectations came alive. The crowds were so great that he could stir an entire city (Matthew 21:10). With a play on words, one can say that mission for Jesus was "pure" politics. He had no illusions about not being involved in power and loyalties.

But the exploding expectations were a critical dilemma for Jesus. A movement soon arose to force him to be a king like others (John 6:15). This pinpoints the difficulty for Jesus to associate his mission with a kingdom. He made it clear that the promised new age was becoming reality (Luke 11:20). That was the whole idea of the good news. Jesus talked about the inauguration of God's new reign constantly:

> The Law and the Prophets were proclaimed until John. Since that time, the good news of the kingdom of God is being preached, and everyone is forcing his way into it.
>
> Luke 16:16, NIV.

To think of a king who is ruling without all the usual symbols or structures is not easy (Luke 17:20, 21). It was difficult for Jesus to get across the idea that the God Movement, to use Clarence Jordon's favorite term, is as real and complete as any other kingship on earth.[8] But it operates on radically different principles and values. Jesus kept on preaching it, describing the character of its citizens (Matthew 5—7) and how it would expand and develop as all kingships do—but without the force or violence which others use (Matthew 13).

Jesus patiently kept explaining this unique universal kingdom until his last day on earth. And the disciples kept right on
thinking in the limited national and geographical terms of the
past (Acts 1:3, 6). Hellenists such as Stephen and Paul, with a
more universal worldview, finally could perceive what God was
doing. Stephen's reinterpretation of the Old Testament began the
process. Jesus was seen as a prophet-king like Moses, who was
"both ruler and deliverer," rather than being a king like David
(Acts 7:35, 37).[9]

Jesus and Power

The idea that a king could rule without force and weapons
seemed insane. That was Pilate's taunt: even the temple guards
had more force than Jesus did, so how could he be a king (John
18:33-36)? In a dramatic object lesson—when the judge became
the defendant—Jesus declared that he rules by the power of witness (martyr) to truth, not by military might. The truth and the
sword are incompatible because neither needs the other. The
politics of Jesus organizes power through voluntary commitment
to the truth. He has been the only true radical who has built a
kingship on people-power, without force or violence.

The issue was the same as in Samuel's day: shalom by the
sword or by response to God? John outlined in detail the careful
decision by the Jewish leaders to choose the same option as their
ancestors did a millennium earlier (John 11:45-53). A sellout to
Pax Romana seemed more secure than the way of shalom this
messiah was promoting. That could cause "the whole nation to
perish" and their "holy place to be destroyed!" They could not
trust their salvation to God. (Is our situation today really different?) But, as Jesus cried over the city, they didn't even know
"the things that make for *shalom*" (Luke 19:42).

Jesus believed in power and used it. He was bold and courageous. As I discovered in teaching the Gospels to Buddhists, much
anger and hostility surrounded Jesus (see John 6—8). "Prince of
peace" was an ill-fitting title by our usual concept of peace. Jesus
played with such confusion by saying, "I have not come to bring

shalom, but a sword" (Matthew 10:34). He would create enemies right in one's own home (v. 36), where shalom is most vital. This tension arose with his call for personal response-ability.

The Messiah was just as hardheaded about the hindrances to shalom as the prophets were. He knew that the false visions, hopes, and securities must be broken up and destroyed before the true shalom could rise. His ministry proclaimed deliverance everywhere, freeing people to change allegiances. His evangelism was a powerful and threatening call. To both Jewish and Roman leaders, Jesus presented the same claim as Moses: "Let my people go!" A glimpse into Christ's self-understanding of this mission came in these terms:

> But if it is by the finger of God that I cast out demons, then the kingdom of God has come upon you. When a strong man, fully armed, guards his own palace, his goods are in *shalom*; but when one stronger than he assails him and overcomes him, he takes away his armor in which he trusted, and divides his spoil.
>
> *Luke 11:20-22.*

Jesus deliberately upset the false shalom of Jews and Romans alike; he disregarded traditions and roles, sided with the poor and oppressed, and lived with a free spirit in a lifestyle of integrity. The political impact was so drastic that the leaders saw "the whole world" changing allegiance to him (John 12:19, NIV). No wonder the prince of shalom aroused so much animosity. His mission was to break up the bondage of the false so that the rule of God could be accepted.

One also can see a conscious use of power in the way Jesus organized the disciples into a living movement. Much of his mission time and energy was devoted to the teaching and training of his followers in different levels of leadership—here the inner three, there the twelve, at times the seventy, and sometimes a multitude. He sent out bands of followers, spreading the same ministry in every direction. It was a small beginning, but Jesus' trust was in a dynamic movement that would grow to cover the earth.

"To This You Are Called"

While Jesus was a strong and powerful person, he was known as a kind and gentle man. He showed special concern for women, children, and outcasts. He taught his followers the same traits of humility, sensitivity, and tenderness toward all who respond genuinely. This spirit permeated both his message and his method. Jesus could express deep feelings openly—both tough love and passionate anger—and remain true to himself in total integrity.

The master was free to tell it like it was, responding in terms of the attitudes and reactions of the listener. But he would have nothing to do with manipulation or coercion. The sons of thunder discovered his high regard for the right of persons to reject (Luke 9:55). He respected a decisive yes or no based on a clear awareness of the meaning of God's rule in life.

Thus, Jesus discouraged some would-be followers in whom he sensed reservations or insincerity. Not only did Christ seek for a voluntary decision by each follower, he wanted a carefully weighed and deliberate response. He showed awareness of the critical nature of commitment for covenant relationship.[10] The parable of the sower gives profound insight into the nature of evangelism and the types of response that can be discouraged or avoided.

Just as clearly, Jesus opposed the use of force for destructive purposes. He taught his followers to respond to violence and threats in positive, nonviolent ways, with readiness to suffer hardship, abuse, and even death for his sake.

> But I say to you, Love your enemies and pray for those who persecute you, so that you may be sons of your Father who is in heaven.
>
> *Matthew 5:44ff.*

Such a stance is possible only in God's agape-love, which Jesus modeled from the cross: "Father, forgive them" (Luke 23:34). But it is so essential to the new covenant that Jesus called it his new commandment: "Love one another as I have loved you" (John 13:34, 35; 15:12, 17). In his manual of citizenship, Jesus

declared the shalom-makers to be God's children, for in blessing
our revilers and loving our enemies we are like God (Matthew 5:9-
12, 38-48). William Klassen writes:

> As far as we know, Jesus was the only one who went about
> gathering the "children of peace." Of them he made peacemakers.
> Here a term which for Josephus had the standard designation of
> one who pacifies the land, namely, a general, became important
> for Jesus. For he saw his disciples as following him in reconciling
> people with God and with each other. The later church saw this
> clearly when they used the same term to describe both Jesus as
> peacemaker (Colossians 1:20) and the disciples.
> *Matthew 5:9; Luke 10:6.*[11]

The open arms of the cross are the primary symbol of the
new covenant of shalom. The cross is the sign of reconciliation—
that God's stance in the present age is only and always one of de-
siring restoration—as portrayed by the prodigal's father (Luke
15:20ff.). This stance of outreaching love becomes our own mission as we respond. Everyone who becomes a part of God's new
creation is a participant in God's ongoing ministry of reconciliation (2 Corinthians 5:16-21).

To fulfill that mission, it is necessary to resist all use of violent
force. When he was arrested Jesus struggled with the temptation
to use the Zealot's methods, which Peter expected him to use. But
Jesus had struggled to victory through submission while praying
in Gethsemane. He disarmed Peter with the declaration that he
was choosing God's way of suffering rather than the way of the
sword (John 18:11).

There were other options. At that moment, 72,000 angels
were ready should Jesus declare holy war (Matthew 26:53). That
was the Zealot expectation, and it would have resulted in God's
immediate triumph. But there would be no new covenant and no
shalom for us. God's shalom is possible only if it is incarnated and
offered in the person-to-person context of daily life through the
outreaching spirit of the cross. "The blood of the martyrs is the
seed of the church" because only in such a godlike stance can love
become real, forgiveness believable, and hostility melt away.

But this lesson of how to "walk in his paths" is hard. Jesus had tried to convince his star pupil that God does not operate by the sword. His appeal that violence only causes more violence (Matthew 26:52) likely reminded Peter of an earlier saying: Fighting to save one's life was a sure way to lose it. The context of Christ's call for crossbearing was Peter's determination to use force to save the movement. The Synoptics agree on the definite sequence of that teaching: Peter's confession of Christ, Jesus' prediction of death, Peter's rejection of suffering, and then Jesus' call: "If anyone would come after me, he must deny himself and take up his cross and follow me" (Matthew 16:24; Mark 8:34; Luke 9:23, NIV).

Not only was Peter told that his desire to use weapons in God's service was unacceptable, it would actually put him on the side against God (Matthew 16:23).[12] But Peter couldn't see it. So the patient teacher set up a final exam in Gethsemane (Luke 22:38), allowing Peter to fail miserably in order to learn God's way.

Peter learned that lesson so well that he wrote the major New Testament treatise on how God's covenant people relate to evil, injustice, and violence (1 Peter 2:11—4:19).[13] Whether the injustice is from governments, economics, family, or society, Peter called for Christians to suffer in the same way Jesus did. The divine principle of operation—the just for the unjust (3:18)—is as true for us as for God. Twice Peter insisted that such a stance in life is the very thing to which "you have been called" (2:21; 3:9).

Renouncing the world's way of operation and following the steps of Jesus in suffering love is the substance of salvation.[14] Jesus said repeatedly that only in showing mercy and forgiveness to others do we affirm that we know God's mercy and forgiveness ourselves (Matthew 5:7; 6:12, 15; 18:35). A number of the parables reinforce the point.

God has no other mission in this covenant-of-shalom age. New Testament peacemaking is not *a part of* the gospel—which can be separated if not wanted; it is the gospel. The good news is that hostilities are absorbed, enemies are loved, debts are forgiven, and prodigals are accepted in the community where God rules. This is how shalom on earth becomes a living reality wherever God is King.

◦ ◦ ◦

**Shalom is the power of allegiance (worship) . . .
devoted to God in submission to his rule . . .
in faithfulness (martyr) to the truth.**

9

The Wholeness

Finding Well-Being in
Our Life Together

This is the message God sent to the people of Israel, telling
the good news of *shalom* through Jesus Christ, who is Lord of all
. . . how God anointed Jesus of Nazareth with the Holy Spirit and
power, and how he went around doing good and healing all who
were under the power of the devil, because God was with him.

Acts 10:36, 38, NIV.

That Peter used shalom language to explain the meaning of
Christ's life for the first Gentile followers is quite significant. For
this remarkable summary he joined two different prophetic visions: the good news of shalom and salvation associated with
God's rule and presence (Isaiah 52:7) and the promises of well-being, health, healing, security, and prosperity God made to Israel
(Jeremiah 33:6-9). His words also recall the ministry of healing
and making whole predicted in Isaiah 53:5.

Peter's interpretation meant that the angelic proclamation of
shalom on earth at Jesus' birth was not a false declaration. The
echo of the crowds at the other end of Jesus' life, "*shalom* in
heaven" (Luke 19:38), is equally affirmed in Peter's key words:
"God was with him." The saving action of God was seen again in
the same visible, concrete forms associated with the good life of
shalom.

This simple report of Jesus' mission as going about "doing

good and healing" is an impressive way to speak of extending shalom. It captures the heart of the Messiah—both his life and work—and confirms the powerful anticipations voiced in the songs of Mary and Zechariah at the time of his birth: filling the hungry with good things, guiding our feet in the paths of shalom (Luke 1:53, 79).

These are some of the ways in which the New Testament identifies and associates the salvation which Jesus brought. In chapter 8 we examined the one half of Christ's mission—the political thrust of proclaiming and living under God's rule. Now we turn to the other half of the Gospels' report (Matthew 4:23; Luke 9:11)—a social thrust of restoring persons and society in the new humanity. This is the effect of God's rule on earth.

A Healing/Saving Community

John the Baptist stirred an air of expectancy among the crowds. He identified his message with the level-road, straight-path righteousness of the prophets. He denounced the anti-shalom elements of his day in the tradition of the prophets, speaking directly to the people involved regarding justice. He called for an end to violence and oppression, while advocating open sharing of economic resources (Luke 3:10-14). People's hopes began to rise as they thought this may be "the Christ" (3:15). That sounded like the age of shalom foretold by the prophets.

Luke's account of Jesus' ministry begins on the same note. The text for Jesus' first sermon in his hometown was carefully chosen to identify him and his work with the shalom visions (4:18, 19). The passage selected was one dealing explicitly with social restoration and well-being. It promised physical, emotional, and social healing of infirmities, oppression, and injustice. It sided with the poor and proclaimed jubilee, the remission of debts and the liberation of slaves, which John H. Yoder says were at the center of the theology of Jesus.[1]

Jesus stopped reading right in the middle of the Isaiah 61:2 passage. He did not continue with the latter part of the passage dealing with "the day of vengeance." On the other hand, he stunningly made this shalom vision his own mission with the words: "Today this scripture is fulfilled in your hearing" (Luke 4:21, NIV).

The mission is stated even more dramatically a bit later in Jesus' own terms. The Baptist asked Jesus to identify himself clearly, since John had reason to question if the prophecies were really being fulfilled. Jesus' response was to point to what he was doing for the blind, lame, diseased, deaf, dead, and poor (Luke 7:22, 23). These were the touchstones of his saving mission. He had come to bring wholeness and well-being to those who least expected it.

The clash of anticipations was already obvious and painful. Any burly Galilean could "proclaim freedom for the prisoners" by raiding prisons. (That would have been the more natural way to interpret Isaiah 61:1.) But only this Galilean could bring wholeness to crippled bodies, captive minds, and depressed spirits. Creating a radically new society was something that only the power and presence of God among the people could do. This was the meaning of the message for John.

The message also meant that Jesus would leave the Baptist to perish in the dungeon. Jesus had power, yet he had to turn his back on his own cousin. He left him with only a prayer: that John would be able to perceive what God was really about and not lose faith (Luke 7:23). The shalom-justice established by the Messiah was far deeper and more threatening than any Zealot violence.

Jesus fulfilled his mission by returning to the prophetic view of God's rule on earth and empowering people to respond to it. He freed persons from every bondage. His "exoduses" included release from fears, chaos, traditions, brokenness, and indebtedness. Once again shalom was real enough to see and feel. His invitation was "Come and see;" his blessing was "Go in shalom."

The Gospels seem to overdramatize the extent of the healing work. Matthew repeated a summary statement that sounds like a typical news report:

Jesus went about all the cities and villages, teaching in their

synagogues and preaching the gospel of the kingdom, and healing
every disease and every infirmity.
Mastthew 9:35; cf. 4:23.

Luke affirmed that "great multitudes gathered to hear and
to be healed of their infirmities" (Luke 5:15). Three times Luke
identified the healing ministry of Jesus with "the power of the
Lord" being with him (5:17; 6:19; 8:46). This led to the bold declaration that this healing, freeing power was proof that God's rule
had begun (11:20).

Christ's ministry of making whole should be seen in the
larger motif of shalom. He indeed felt compassion for the suffering of people. But his use of power also countered chaos and established order. The miracles were signs that God was in control,
turning disorder and confusion into harmony and wholeness. This
was symbolized in drama by stilling the storm with the appeal,
"*Shalom*" (Mark 4:39). The change was just as dramatic for the
confusion, wailing, and mocking in Jairus' house (5:38-42) or in
the midst of the weeping, despair, and stench of the Lazarus
event (John 11).

A Sharing Community

Healing also ties into the themes of deliverance, freedom,
and newness that are associated with shalom. These aspects are
seen in Jesus' teaching on economics, where the healing of broken
relations and shattered dreams is so sorely needed. In keeping
with the economic concerns of the prophets' judgments and their
visions, possessions and money were dominant topics for Jesus.
The Messiah was expected to take a firm stance on the cause of so
much misery and woe.

Jesus understood the close connection between violence and
possessions. He knew that the greater the accumulation of wealth,
the more anxiety it brings and the more law and order is required
to protect it. Laying up "treasures on earth" simply challenges the
thieves to "break in and steal" (Matthew 6:19). The call of Jesus
to nonviolence was interspersed with an equal call to sharing and
mutuality (5:38-42). The two ideals go hand-in-hand, for economic injustice is already a form of violence.

How was "good news to the poor" a validation of messianic claims? It revealed God's concern for the poor and those with special needs. They were drawn to Jesus like a magnet. He had to refuse the temptation to provide daily manna for the crowds. Another wilderness experience must have looked appealing to "all who labor and are heavy laden" (Matthew 11:28; 4:3; John 6:15, 26).

But again the broader picture suggests that in denouncing the economic oppression and siding with the poor, Jesus was standing in the line of the prophets. The anger he expressed in clearing and opening the temple courts was a powerful illustration of how deeply he felt. Wherever poverty and riches exist side-by-side, there is lack of justice, fidelity, and shalom. The will and rule of God, who has created enough for all, is being thwarted. The Lord sends the rain and sunshine on the just and unjust alike (Matthew 5:45).

Jesus believed that the earth offered abundant resources for all. What is missing is the spirit and practice of jubilee. Jesus and his followers lived out the ancient shalom oracle which anticipated a vine and fig tree for every person (Micah 4:4). Actually, the new messianic community was more like Zechariah's addition to the dream:

> "In that day each of you will invite his neighbor to sit under his vine and fig tree," declares the Lord Almighty.
>
> *Zechariah 3:10, NIV.*

So Jesus insisted that a heavenly Father who feeds the sparrows and clothes the grass is surely able to supply our needs as well. He did not hesitate to offer the same security and prosperity which God had promised in the old covenant. His followers were told that if they keep their priorities fixed on God's rule and will, then "all these things will be given to you as well" (Matthew 6:33, NIV).

The promise was spelled out in astonishing detail. Jesus offered 100 times more houses, lands, and family "now in this time" than anyone gives up for the movement. Eternal life in the age to come is the bonus (Mark 10:29, 30; Luke 18:29, 30). Do not overlook the detail which Mark adds, "with persecutions." Jesus was realistic. Just as the Baptist had to find his shalom in prison, so the disciples would experience their shalom in the midst of the same violence to which Jesus was subjected (Matthew 10:21, 22).

The setting for the above offer was the encounter with the rich, young ruler. (We tend to emphasize what he could not give up instead of what he forfeited.) The discussion which followed indicates that Jesus had offered him more, not less. The offer was clarified in response to Peter's puzzlement. The disciples had done just what the Master asked of the young leader; but they had not seen the promised rewards and wondered, "What then shall we have?" (Matthew 19:27).

One of my lowest moments overseas came when a pastor from the mountains of northern Luzon (Philippines) stopped me in class as I was expounding rather glibly on Matthew 6:33. The rugged barrio captain stood up and read Matthew 19:27. In a soft, wistful voice he said, "Brother James, my question is exactly the same as Peter's." Then he sat down and I squirmed. I clearly recall staring out of the bus window on the long journey home that evening, wondering if I really had anything to say to Brother Balucos, for we both knew that sometimes he had no rice in the house for his family.

I have decided since then that kingdom promises should be read only by kingdom citizens living in kingdom communities. They were not meant for individuals living private lifestyles. The economic sayings of Jesus (as well as his standards of nonviolence) make sense only in the context of a group fully committed to each other, living a common life in the spirit of shalom, under God's rule. Such ideals require trust and mutuality in the community of the Spirit amid life's uncertainties.

This was precisely the new community created by Jesus. Its members, upon returning from their missions, testified that they never lacked anything (Luke 22:35). Once the sharing community got into full operation after the coming of the Spirit, Peter never again wondered about his hundredfold reward—or what was in it for him.

For us to comprehend "the good news" which a proclamation of jubilee would be to slaves and laborers indebted for life is
hard. Most likely when we pray the Lord's Prayer we don't even
think of real debts or loans. But Jesus was insistent that only those
who practice jubilee on earth will receive jubilee from heaven
(Matthew 5:7; 6:14, 15). The debt of the un-jubilant servant
remained when he revealed that he didn't believe in mercy or in
canceling debts (Matthew 18:21-35). The purpose of jubilee is to
re-create a totally new situation for a fresh start in life and relationships.[2]

A Caring Community

In terms of where Jesus put his energies and concern, the
formation of the shalom community was the prime objective of
his mission. He spent the major portion of his time forming a
people who would covenant together to live daily in the spirit and
guidelines of shalom. Their loyalty to the movement and to the
welfare of each other had the intensity of complete abandonment.
Peter spoke for the group in declaring that they had all done what
the young ruler refused: "We have left all we had to follow you!"
(Luke 18:28, NIV).

This was the dynamite of Christ's approach in calling
followers committed to a totally new orientation in life. He
molded disciples in the classical student-master tradition. The
students learned by patterning their daily lives, attitudes, and
values after their master. By focusing on a new way of life in community, the basic concerns of shalom for just and right relationships were natural in the God Movement. In learning the
ways of God, these followers were recapturing the original intention for life—the more abundant life (John 10:10).

The daily life of Jesus and his followers is not described in the
Gospels in the same detail as the Jerusalem fellowship is in Acts.
But the glimpses we have suggest great similarity. The breaking
of bread together must have been a daily celebration of their common life, expressing a sense of covenant and fellowship (see Luke
24:30, 35). Jesus obviously enjoyed eating with others, even at

large banquets. With the sharing of a meal together such a key element of both covenant and shalom, it was no coincidence that the Lord's supper became the primary symbol of the new covenant of shalom.

Some have said that the experiences following the Holy Spirit's coming were ecstatic expressions of newness and joy which proved to be rather impractical. Acts 2 and 4 describe the sense of community in glowing terms that evoke flashbacks of Eden. Peter declared, "This is it," as he cited the prophets' dreams about the wonderful things they were seeing and feeling.

Luke began the book of Acts by referring to his Gospel which tells what "Jesus began to do and teach" (Acts 1:1). The master had modeled and taught how they were to live. The disciples were not trying something new. They were simply continuing the lifestyle and economics which their Lord had lived among them during his ministry.[3] The excitement of their evangelism arose largely from their living out those wild dreams of shalom. That was heady and contagious ferment—social dynamite.

The disciples likely perceived the year of jubilee which Jesus had announced as an ongoing characteristic of the new covenant of shalom. Instinctively they must have sensed in the jubilee spirit the greatest expression of joyful koinonia they could imagine. Norman Kraus says they were moved to fulfill the highest perception of commonality found in the Torah.[4] They certainly saw themselves continuing to declare the good news of God's kingship (Acts 14:22; 19:8; 28:23). And it would have seemed most fitting in the dawn of the shalom age that any resource should be available for any need.

The expressions of mutuality were attractively clear. In the descriptions of their life together (2:43ff.; 4:32ff.) two motifs are sharply contrasted: *idios* (private, self-centered, or other "idiotic" interests) and *koinos* (public, shared, or held in common). It is quite obvious which was considered as the essence of the new community. How extremely parallel these two motifs are to all we have learned about shalom and anti-shalom.

The breaking of bread together became the daily expression

of the shared life the new community enjoyed. The open table of food and worship was a significant sign of the new age:

> They broke bread in their homes and ate together with glad and sincere hearts, praising God and enjoying the favor of all the people.
>
> *Acts 2:46b, 47a, NIV.*

This was a daily celebration of "the new humanity" created in Christ Jesus. It is the original portrait of salvation in the new covenant—described in Ephesians 2 as the forming of one new body, doing away with the anti-shalom elements of division, alienation, and hostility. Shalom had come to earth; fulfillment of God's mission had begun.

As we read of The Way spreading out to other cities and peoples, we do not see any rigid practice or fixed pattern of daily life in the koinonia of the Spirit. But we do see the same spirit of commonality and caring expressed in various ways (Romans 12:13; 2 Corinthians 8:2-4; Hebrews 13:16). James pointed to the irony of saying, "*Shalom,*" be warmed and filled," to a person lacking clothes and food (James 2:14ff.). He was specific about what makes or breaks shalom (3:13—4:4), declaring that there can be no faith in God where there is no caring, sharing spirit among the people. John set this contradiction in a haunting question:

> But if anyone has the world's goods and sees his brother in need, yet closes his heart against him, how does God's love abide in him?
>
> *1 John 3:17.*

A Restoring Community

These warnings from James and John remind us of "flies in the ointment." As the parable of the sower illustrates, God's mission must still contend with a mixture of motives and degrees of commitment. The New Testament is as realistic about anti-shalom elements and tendencies as the Old. Continuing the Genesis tradition, the New Testament makes no effort to hide or belittle the failures sustained.

So the tragic deaths of Judas in the shadow of the cross and of Ananias and Sapphira in the celebration of Pentecost confront us with this startling awareness. The struggles of Cain and Abel and Jacob and Esau now are seen right "in the Garden" of the new age. The enemies of shalom—disloyalty and hypocrisy, greed and unbelief—lurk in the midst of our highest joy and achievement. Acts 5 suggests that the ideal which so attracts us, by its demand of full commitment, may create the very pitfall that imprisons us anew.

These incidents highlight the seriousness with which one's commitment to the group was viewed. Broken pledges had to be dealt with, since shalom required faithfulness and integrity. Although Peter was told not to count the times his brother or sister needed forgiveness, the context of that teaching is how to discipline an unrepentant member (Matthew 18:15-22). This direct confrontation of wrongdoing keeps the group discipled and loyal.

This "binding and loosing" through group process and discernment is one aspect of the early church often overlooked today. No health and wholeness for the group can exist without clear expectations and accountability, including ways to deal with failure and disruption. In association with this vital function of the community's life Jesus gave the promise of his presence—even if only two or three persons take their covenants seriously (Matthew 18:20).

The directives in Matthew 18 for the restoration of shalom show that unfaithfulness and disharmony in the web of relationship threatens the life of the group. Action must be taken to safeguard the shalom and allow its dynamic for growth to function. The excommunication called for as the last resort is a visible expression of the estrangement already felt in the group's spirit. It is done for the sole purpose of winning the offender back into fellowship as any other uncommitted person.[5]

The focus of concern is not for purity *per se* but for healing of a fractured group. Restoration is the objective, as Paul put it:

Brethren, if a man is overtaken in any trespass, you who are

spiritual should restore him in a spirit of gentleness. Look to yourself, lest you too be tempted.

Galatians 6:1.

Yet if the person chooses not to be reconciled, then for the order
and solidarity of the group, that choice must be officially
recognized.[6]

Shalom requires mutually freeing and uplifting interpersonal
relationships. This is where shalom often faces its greatest test.
The Gospels detail the build-up of conflicts among the disciples,
calling forth Christ's teachings about greatness and servanthood.
The more Jesus spoke of following the way of the suffering
servant, the more the twelve argued about rank and prestige. One
sees how the attitudes of each member towards self and others determine the degree of shalom for the group.

The disciples illustrate the critical balance between individual and community. Neither the person nor the group can
function fully without a healthy respect which maintains the importance of both. The desire and tendency to put one's own rights
and interests ahead of a neighbor's must be denied for the commonality needed for shalom. Jesus opposed all titles and practices
that fostered divisions and jealousies. Slaves and children were his
models. His own spirit expressed the same traits of unassuming
genuineness without airs or prejudices.

Only in such an atmosphere will acceptance be natural and
forgiveness come readily. No true shalom can exist without these
graces and spirit, for we all do offend, trespass, and fail (Luke
17:1-4; Galatians 6:1). The shalom of any group will be tested and
shaken. What is new in the good news is that, through God's
example of love and mercy, we can confront problems and find
healing. Shalom is not the opposite of conflict; rather, it is the use
of differences and confrontation to facilitate new growth and
creativity.

Relationships in the covenant of shalom are not as harmonious as were those in Eden. Jesus had to work patiently with his
followers, dealing with their rivalries and jealousies. Yet in a brief

time he molded a collection of diverse individuals into a close-knit, caring group, strong enough to withstand the trauma of their founder's rejection and death with only one casualty. They carried the mission on together, not smoothly or perfectly, but experiencing enough to keep the vision alive.

We can do the same today. But our shalom must be hardheaded enough to deal with the realities of life and our imperfect efforts. To ignore the fatal potential of our anti-shalom tendencies is to relinquish our hopes and longings. Our shalom also must be softhearted enough to respond to every need, encouraging every desire to live by God's order. Anything less than the spirit of forgiving "seventy times seven" (Matthew 18:22) negates the vision to which we aspire. For shalom comes to each person wherever she or he is at, nudging one step at a time towards God's intention.

o o o

**Shalom is the invitation to be truly whole. . .
celebrating the good life with sisters and brothers
who are covenanted together for the well-being of all.**

SHALOM IS OUR MISSION TOO

10

Shalom Is Mission

*T*his has been a brief survey of one of the most complex and comprehensive motifs of the Scriptures. We are only beginning to grasp the force of this driving vision of God in biblical history. Recent scholarship is enabling us to see shalom as one of the most formative principles shaping the Old Testament record. But little has been done to follow the same influence through the New Testament era. Somehow it seems easier to be thrilled with the shalom dreams of the prophets than with the fulfillment in the messianic age to which they pointed.

We need to allow this study of God's mission to critique the way we are going about our missions. Do our missions reflect that we truly believe the Messiah has come and ushered in the new "covenant of shalom" as foretold? To what extent do our life and message mirror those anticipations of what God wants to do in the world? Or have we given up the vision simply because others have spurned it? Do we give up the entire shalom-mission just because we can't expect the final stages of perfection in this world?

We seem to have reduced the ecstatic images of messianic salvation to a peephole view of God's intentions for the people of the new covenant. The self-fulfilling expectations we have accepted of our situation have forced us to talk either of pie-in-the-sky or some golden millennium in the future. If Jesus were to appear today, would he have a message different from his call to repentance in response to God's rule?

To begin relating this study of shalom more directly to mission, we will go back to the first text on Christian missions, Luke 10. Though we have read it often, it may be that we have never really heard Jesus tell his followers to fulfill their mission by offering to live in shalom with their listeners. How could Jesus describe evangelism as simply saying "Shalom" to others?

Missions have not paid much attention to this original model. Should the founder of a movement not be allowed to shape the way that mission is to be perceived and continued by his future followers? I suspect that one reason for not taking Christ's words more seriously is that it did not mean anything to us to be told, "Go and say, 'Shalom'!" That is no longer an excuse.

To give careful attention to Luke 10 does not mean that we should obey the instructions in a literal or legalistic manner. We want to look at how the disciples would have understood their directives, which mirror the spirit and concern of Jesus' own mission. We will note examples from the book of Acts showing that the early church took the principles and concerns of the text seriously—but with flexibility.

The Spirit of Mission

After this the Lord appointed seventy others, and sent them on ahead of him, two by two, into every town and place where he himself was about to come. And he said to them, "The harvest is plentiful, but the laborers are few; pray therefore the Lord of the harvest to send out laborers into his harvest. Go your way; behold, I send you out as lambs in the midst of wolves. Carry no purse, no bag, no sandals; and salute no one on the road."

Luke 10:1-4.

The four opening verses of this treatise on missions form a context vital for the realization of the shalom-mission. Jesus was concerned first and foremost with the spirit and attitude of his missioners. The how and the what were viewed as equally critical for effective communications. He showed an awareness that the message is inseparably tied to the means. In both life and teaching, Jesus was deliberate in the method and spirit used in missions.

First, we read that the seventy[1] were appointed for a specific task. They were given a definite purpose and goal. They even must have had a schedule to follow, since the record says later that they all "returned with joy" (Luke 10:17). A clear commission meant that the seventy knew who they were and what they were about. Their instructions were explicit.

Why the strategy of sending them "two by two," especially while praying for more laborers who are needed in the great harvest? Jesus apparently viewed thirty-five teams of two people each to be more effective than seventy isolated individuals. This was true even for the brief assignment he projected.

Jesus likely recognized the human need for companionship and support (as in Eden). His instructions may also reflect his insight into the nature of the gospel witness. A team could express and model the new community, with a nucleus on which to build wherever they went. This is crucial when we see the emphasis given to living the gospel in Jesus' strategy. This symbol of mutuality would be the first thing a village would notice. The missionary teams of Acts show how well the early church understood this principle.

Second, "the Lord of the harvest" commissioned them. His first appeal and task was for them to pray to him. A spirit of prayerful concern for the harvest in which they were to participate was prerequisite. Instead of drumming up confidence that they could easily complete the task, Jesus created a sense of dependence on the Lord of the harvest. Both needed more harvesters. But one Lord sending laborers into one harvest for one purpose also spoke of a mutuality that left no place for a competitive spirit.

The image of harvest added an eschatological note to the context of the mission. Those responding to Christ's call were sent as participants in the messianic mission leading to the end of the age. They would be reaping where "others have labored" (John 4:35-38). The image also suggested that their work as harvesters is related to the judgment and ultimate purpose of the world.

But, third, lest that awareness evoke a haughty spirit of

power and prestige, Jesus hastened to fix an unmistakable image: they were being sent "as lambs in the midst of wolves." In Matthew's report of these instructions, Jesus added two more images to reinforce the point:

So be wise as serpents and innocent (gentle) as doves *(10:16)*.

To miss the point is hard, especially when Luke places these words just ten verses after Jesus had to rebuke his followers for wanting to call fire from heaven on those rejecting their witness. Jesus knew that a high and holy calling tends to make people act like high and mighty ambassadors.

Lambs and doves are certainly not the characterizations usually associated with missionaries of the modern missionary movement, which in nearly every case has been associated with the expansion of colonial powers. Certainly the Vietnamese had plenty of reason to believe—in both the French and American eras—that the Western missionaries were associated with the rain of fire from the skies.

We will reflect a bit later on the importance of a lamblike spirit to mission as defined and modeled by Jesus. Having lived with this illicit relationship of the word and the sword for over 1600 years, the church cannot see how totally incongruous it is to preach the cross in the shadow of the cannon.[2] In the end we all look like wolves. But the lamb of God prayed:

As thou didst send me into the world, so I have sent them into the world.
John 17:18; 20:21.

With all the fearless confrontation and dramatic strength that Jesus showed, there was no question whether he was a lamb or a wolf. He fulfilled Isaiah's portrait of a messiah who would not even break off a bent reed, though he persists until justice triumphs. Jesus called for the same spirit in his missioners to go with their message of shalom.

In the fourth place, the vulnerability required by the lamb

and dove images is sharpened even more by a stance of dependency. Jesus sent the seventy on their mission without money or baggage. These instructions were changed later when they were faced with a hostile situation on the eve of his death (Luke 22:36). However, the book of Acts indicates a fairly literal observance of this approach. Years later Paul wrote:

> Do we not have the right to our food and drink?. . . The Lord commanded that those who proclaim the gospel should get their living by the gospel.
> *1 Corinthians 9:4, 14.*

Those who have lived among the missionary barrels know that these too are hard words. We are shaped by a consumer-driven, comfort-crazed, instant-everything American society. The contrast between the typical U.S. missionary and our Buddhist counterparts in Vietnam was as striking in the realm of possessions and material values as in the matter of force and violence. No one dared to ask who looked more like Jesus.

We know it is possible to live a "daily bread" lifestyle for which Jesus taught us to pray in childlike faith. But we are so far from the lifestyle of Jesus, or Gandhi, or millions in the world today that I wonder why we keep praying the Lord's Prayer. Jesus knew, however, that we can't risk saying shalom in covenant with another person without the anxiety-free attitudes and jubilee values of Matthew 5, 6, and 7. That is why this prologue in Luke 10 is so critical. The shalom-mission asks more than most of us have even considered.

The spiraling use of and dependence on technology in all of its dimensions merely heightens this dilemma for missions. Americans seem enamored by gadgets and machines. I confess that it is much easier to point to the problem than to the solution. Yet many mission workers fail to see any problem or inconsistency. As long as programs have top priority, we will need our technology and systems to carry them out. In settings such as Vietnam, those needs made us highly dependent on the military-governmental networks for logistics and protection.

Evangelism Is Extending Shalom

> Whatever house you enter, first say, "*Shalom* be to this house!" And if a son of *shalom* is there, your *shalom* shall rest upon him; but if not, it shall return to you.
>
> *Luke 10:5, 6.*

After carefully describing the spirit and attitudes Jesus expects in his missionaries, he tells them how to carry out their mission. The instructions are brief and clear; the method is direct and open. The followers of Jesus later spoke of him fulfilling his own mission in precisely this way. Peter spoke of God "preaching good news of *shalom* by Jesus Christ" (Acts 10:36). Paul's summation of the Lord's mission was similar:

> And he came and preached *shalom* to you who were far off and *shalom* to those who were near.
>
> *Ephesians 2:17.*

How could Jesus tell the seventy to carry out their mission by simply saying "Shalom" to their hearers? To catch the potential of this missiology, we need to draw on all the insights about this concept which we noted in Section Two. Instead of asking what shalom has to do with mission (already quite fixed in our minds), we should discern the kind of mission that can be defined and fulfilled by offering shalom to a stranger.

First of all, to say "Shalom" in this way is to offer a meaningful commitment. Jesus was not suggesting that his followers give friendly greetings. Notice that he was specific about contextualization. They were to offer shalom to the household only upon entering the house.

The contrast to this observation appears in verse 4: "Do not greet anyone on the road" (NIV). Since shalom is established by creating a web of trusting and harmonious relationships, was Jesus implying that it cannot be done "on the road"? The kind of evangelism Jesus was prescribing requires more than a passing encounter. The context required for shalom suggests certain limitations in regards to methods and strategy.

The word of shalom is to be spoken in the familiar, everyday setting of the strangers' home. That immediately calls for a standard of straight talk, an openness to close scrutiny, and a readiness for interaction. It takes the gospel right to the place where shalom needs to begin. Jesus' concern for demonstrated validity, expressed in his come-and-see invitation, is brought right to the unbeliever's own turf.

Jesus is asking for high-level risk and deep vulnerability. Saying "Shalom" to a stranger in his or her home symbolizes a willingness to "throw my life in with yours." Saying "Shalom" purposefully means to offer a peace treaty, a pledge to live for the other's well-being, a covenant to desire and seek the good life of God's favor together. This is Christ's definition of evangelism. No wonder shalom-mission needs more than casual contacts along the way where it would have no context for meaning.

Second, to do evangelism by extending shalom to others is to take God's stance visibly in the world. It confronts the rebellious, hostile world in the out-reaching, open-armed stance of the cross. It embodies and expresses in life and actions the message of reconciliation that we have been entrusted with as ambassadors for Christ. To say "Shalom" to another person in the name of Christ is the New Testament mission:

> So we are ambassadors for Christ, God making his appeal through us. We beseech you on behalf of Christ, be reconciled to God.
>
> *2 Corinthians 5:20.*

As the heavenly messengers offered "*shalom* on earth" to the fearful shepherds that night the shalom prince was born, so the same good news is to be graciously proclaimed to every home that welcomes God's messengers. This is the opening appeal of God's mission: past, present, and future.

All who respond to that offer are by its nature commissioned to pass it on. As with mercy and forgiveness, we lack the proof of ever receiving the shalom of God if we are not sharing the same with others. For no person whose enmity and alienation has been melted away by hearing God say "Shalom" can withhold the same loving acceptance from others who are still fighting.

Offering shalom to enemies is what the gospel is all about. Can anyone question that mission must be concerned for and involved with peace concerns? Death on the cross is the proof of how deeply God feels about extending shalom to a rebelling people. Apart from such love we would not dare to lay down our arms in surrender. Only convincing, sacrificial love can confront and disarm those opposing God's will in the world. That is the only way we can believe that God is truly for us.

Jesus charged those who had responded to his mission to embody the same to others in his stead. They were to "go and say *Shalom*" to friends and foe alike just as he was doing. We seem to have convinced ourselves that today's national interests, political issues, materialistic values, or educated awareness have turned our mission into a different creature. But has the divine mission really changed?

A third impression this passage makes upon us about shalom evangelism is its two-way communication process. After the offer is made, one must be silent and listen for acceptance or rejection. The invitation to shalom demands a response.

Once as I was speaking about shalom, I suddenly realized that I wasn't sure how to say the word as a covenant offer. Is it a question ("Shalom?") or a declaration ("Shalom!")? It is, of course, a question or conditional offer in that it calls for a reply. That is the two-way dimension. One cannot make a shalom pact alone. The nature of shalom is to reach out and interact with others in ever-widening circles. It constantly desires, calls forth, and builds on the positive responses to its invitation.

That is why Jesus said the mission was finished wherever there was no echo of shalom. He instructed missioners to stay only if there was clear interest and openness to consider living in shalom.

Werner Foerster says it well:

> The greeting they give on entering a house is not a wish. It is a gift which is either received or rejected as such. So real is this that if rejected it returns to the disciples.[3]

Therefore, the offer is made in the form of a question, requiring a similar interest in reconciliation on the part of the listener. Without that spark of desire and sense of need, one can do nothing to bring shalom-salvation to that home.

Nevertheless, shalom must be proclaimed as a declaration of firm intent on the part of the messenger. To be authentic, the person extending God's offer dare have no question or reservation. The representatives of Jesus are to be ready to commit themselves fully and freely to live for the wholeness of those who respond in hope at the sound of the word.

Shalom is a joyful word celebrating goodness and life. So our declaration should ring with hope and anticipation of the favor of God being extended in a wider circle. Everyone who joins the family brings added abilities, resources, and strength to the movement. That is the enthusiasm reflected in the book of Acts.

But note again Jesus' words: "*First* say." Even when we hear the desired response, the missioning process has only begun. The missionary then has an open door for a more specific witness. It's like getting a yes for a first big date in a courtship, with the goal of a marriage covenant yet in the future. The lifelong commitment will come only after a careful, deliberate process. Again we see the strategy discouraging premature decisions.

Blueprint for Shalom Missions

And remain in the same house, eating and drinking what they provide, for the laborer deserves his wages; do not go from house to house. Whenever you enter a town and they receive you, eat what is set before you; heal the sick in it and say to them, "The kingdom of God has come near to you."

Luke 10:7-9.

Jesus continued by giving precise details for development of the witness. His missioners have been welcomed into the house. An interest and receptivity to the gift of shalom has been established. Yet how does the shalom vision become reality and the kingdom-rule of God take effect in a new setting? How is God's will best communicated and discerned?

For Americans who like exact formulas such as three easy steps or four spiritual laws, the body of this original text is most ideal. No need for overhead projectors or copy machines if you can give your instructions in just three short, crisp words. So oddly simplistic are those words that our modern sophistication has probably tripped and skipped them before their profoundness could register. But mission for Jesus really was as simple as eating, healing, and saying—if done in the right spirit and purpose.

1. EAT. Who could imagine a mission strategy beginning with eating—not as an introductory gesture of friendship, but as one third of the whole plan! Yet for the objectives Jesus sought, eating was the vital, beginning stage of a three-part development. It laid the foundation for the success of the entire mission. But Jesus had more in mind than simply enjoying good food or big feasts.

The directive to eat was qualified quickly with a restriction which set forth the purpose. To "eat what is set before you" suggested at once that Jesus was thinking of more than daily nourishment. His disciples would also wash, sleep, and take care of other daily needs without being told. Jesus intended the eating to express symbolically the attitudes, values, and principles that are essential to the mission.

The Lord of the harvest was calling his disciples to complete identification with the people to whom they wanted to witness. To accept the hospitality of a stranger in the Middle East setting had more implications than for most of us today. Entering a house and sitting together at someone's table said a great deal about intentions, trust, and obligations. Eating together would build on the initial openness of the welcome and encourage the hosts to invest more than curiosity in the encounter.

Persons involved with missions will immediately see some familiar principles involved here. Not only are these missionaries meeting on the listeners' home turf, they are beginning on the receptors' own terms. Not only does this strategy require living one's faith openly in their midst, it calls for a bold affirmation of them as valued persons. Such an approach speaks volumes about the respect and esteem given to the people and also to their culture.

In fact, Jesus made it pretty clear that no judgmental attitudes or personal tastes are to offend the graciousness of this moment. Forget cultural differences, moral perspectives, and squeamish stomachs. He had already stated in the previous verse that his missionaries were expected to eat and drink "whatever they give you" (NIV). The would-be giver must first demonstrate how to receive.

Jesus knew from his own experience how to build rapport quickly and earn a hearing. He deliberately created a context of dependency for the missionary by allowing the people to minister first in ways that they easily could. There would be no fostering of paternalism or inferiority around that table of shared bread. Instead of trying to impress the audience with the superiority and power of the missionary, Christ's first step is actually to grant power to the strangers being approached. His tactic was asking the woman at the well for a drink or the lad for his loaves and fish.

We have already noted that eating together is one of the chief symbols of shalom. This is the shalom-mission in action. Feelings of acceptance and belonging begin to stir as these strangers break bread together, putting some reality into that opening invitation to shalom. The sequence starts with an unpretentious social act (exactly where the people are) which leads eventually to the covenantal meal of communion.

In this simple way Jesus brings together two crucial concepts: incarnation and alienation. The primary appeal of such a mission plan is to allow presence to overcome estrangement. It views others as being lost and lonely, needing to belong and be included. The missionary brings an offer of acceptance, reconciliation, and community to people before they are told what's wrong with them. The missionary is to become "one with" those to whom he or she is witnessing, which is the power of identification (incarnation).

Moreover, Jesus sought to develop that new sense of relationship as intensely as possible. We see this in his preliminary counsel: "Remain in the same house . . . do not go from house to house." He did not indicate how long they were to stay, but the plan called for a concentrated encounter: the more exposure, the better the opportunity. Yet this scheme works only as the participants see God truly becoming one of them.

This approach had often been demonstrated by Jesus, so often that it earned him that infamous nickname of "a glutton and a drunkard" (Luke 7:34). What better beginning in the new reality was there for those feeling outcast and rejected? The meals Jesus ate with Matthew and his friends (Mark 2:13ff.) and with Zacchaeus ("for I must stay at your house today," Luke 19:1-10) were tremendous signs of the new order. Such acceptance and affirmation had the prodigals responding in joyful jubilee. But such actions meant consternation and rage to those whose attitudes were reflected by "the elder brother." They did not believe in incarnation.

2. HEAL. Establishing a sense of identity and oneness with the people will result in an awareness of the sufferings and aspirations of the household or town. At that point, identification turns into participation.

The first stage can make the missionary look and feel like a sponger, like Elijah asking the widow of Zarepath for a cake from the last of her meal. Our Lord would not intend for anyone to be a hardship or added burden for needy people. Paul found it wise at times not to follow this approach (1 Corinthians 9:15, 18). The goal is to find the most effective way of gaining the trust and respect of those to whom we are sent as witnesses.

The seventy were not told how long to wait before launching step two. We know that Jesus healed Peter's feverish mother-in-law and Zacchaeus' troubled spirit at the time of the first meal. But not all needs are so visible or obvious. The principle suggests relating to the people's needs as they request or reveal them. A predetermined program often ends up scratching where it doesn't itch. We will be on target if we fulfill step one adequately.

The approach in the second phase is to get involved with the people's experience of anti-shalom. It addresses the brokenness, disease, and oppression from which the people long to be delivered and made whole. That is the natural impulse of anyone offering to live in shalom with such persons. The causes of the anti-shalom must be confronted.

Anyone claiming to represent the compassionate ministry of Jesus cannot sit idly in the presence of needs or suffering that can be alleviated. The heart of the shalom vision is to desire and seek the same well-being for others that I want for myself. The missionary who follows this blueprint for mission has already associated her/his own shalom with this household in the opening declaration. There is no question about participating in their needs when shalom is declared with integrity.

Jesus commissioned his followers to continue the same mission in which he was so fully engaged. What we noted in chapter 9 about the healing and saving ministry of Jesus was applied to the mission carried on by his followers. They were responsible to keep on fulfilling those visions and anticipations of a people being restored to wholeness in the order of God's rule.

Thus, the power to heal and make whole would be the sign of God's ruling presence for the followers just as for Jesus. Remembering that in the Greek language "healing" and "saving" were of the same root word, we need to hear Christ's command to heal and save as encompassing the total work of God among the people. The mission is to make the messianic vision a reality in the life of this household and village.

The come-and-see invitation has been turned into a commissioned go-and-show. The charge of Luke 4:18, 19 is now passed on to these followers, as the parallel passage in Matthew 10:8 makes clear:

Heal the sick, raise the dead, cleanse lepers, cast out demons.

We know from their exuberant report afterward (Luke 10:17) that the seventy overcame the same evil spirits and oppression that Jesus had encountered. They engaged in the same shalom-mission they had seen their master fulfilling.

This involvement in a holistic ministry was continued in the book of Acts. After their first imprisonment, the apostles prayed for boldness to witness, asking the Lord to "stretch out your hand to heal" (4:30; see the result in 5:15, 16, NIV). The account of Philip's preaching and healing ministry in Samaria sounds like Jesus in Galilee, causing "much joy in that city" (8:4-8). One of the closing scenes in the last chapter tells of a shipwrecked Paul taking time to heal the islanders before sailing on with many gifts. He did this in the home of the local chief who had received them with hospitality (28:7-10).

3. SAY. This final step is where many of the missionaries I have observed want to begin. They seem to believe that Jesus had a transposed order and that such priorities are confused. Even in a transcultural setting, they do not share Jesus' concern for preparation through the demonstrated and serving word. I heard missionaries in the midst of Vietnam's desperate need say that preaching was the only thing they were called to do.

But Jesus looked first for the effect of incarnate presence, fleshing out God's will and concern in the midst of the people. This would be followed by a ministry of caring that allowed God to intervene and participate in the personal, human situation. Such involvement showed what it means to live by the shalom-rule of God. Only after the people had seen and felt the meaning of God's presence for them were they ready to hear the good news. Then they could accept or reject the invitation with clear awareness of the significance of either response.

By this time the message can be quite brief and to the point. The seventy were told to say simply: "This is the ruling presence of God. God has come to you in what you are witnessing. This is the shalom being offered by the Lord to us all. Do you want it? Is this the life you are looking for?"

That is the invitation. According to Jesus, preaching is to be an explanation of the new reality people have been observing. It does not require a lot of foreign concepts, mental gymnastics, or religious jargon. It does require a bold, clear declaration that this is the will and intention of God for all people.

The verbal witness is needed to explain and reinforce the living witness. These people have felt God's warm acceptance. They sense a genuine regard as persons of worth and potential. They have seen unconditional love and unselfish service in the name of Christ. The offer of forgiveness and reconciliation has become credible. They need only the word of invitation, but it must be given clearly and convincingly.

Because of the open modeling in the daily life and attitudes of the two-messenger team, the people of this household or village will know what it means to be part of the God-movement. When they respond to the offer, they will not be thinking of giving assent to prescribed beliefs or creedal statements. They will have encountered a vision for life and will be declaring whether they submit to the order on which it is based. It is the King of heaven who now is saying to them: "Shalom!"

So the goal of proclamation is to invite a full and free response to the rule of God. The moment has come when it is no longer enough to observe and participate casually. The time is here to declare intentions and make commitments. The courtship has led to the altar, and it is time for vows. God is calling for an I-thou relationship in the context of the new community.

Covenants made to God in the body of Christ are as binding and significant in life as marriage vows. That is why the call to repentance is a key part of the proclamation. To give complete allegiance to the King and submit to the rule of Christ through our sisters and brothers is the most radical turnabout and reorientation in life. Only sensational terms such as "new birth" and "new creation" can describe the transformation that occurs when one joins this covenant of shalom.

It's Your Choice.

But whenever you enter a town and they do not receive you, go into its streets and say, "Even the dust of your town that clings to our feet, we wipe off against you; nevertheless know this, that the kingdom of God has come near." I tell you, it shall be more tolerable on that day for Sodom than for that town.

Luke 10:10-12.

The Lord was as clear and decisive in dealing with rejection as with acceptance. Witnesses had no need to stay and antagonize when they were not welcomed and received. Nor were they to attempt to bait, manipulate, or force the people for a further hearing or a partial response. Their no was to be heard and respected.

That does not mean that missioners need to slip out the back gate in disgrace (though there were times when the back exit seemed the most suitable, Acts 9:25, 14:6). While Jesus would not allow any thought of punitive action (Luke 9:55), he wanted the fact of rejection to be clearly recognized and openly dramatized. Again, the missionaries in Acts literally "shook the dust off" when faced with opposition in their work (13:51; 18:6; cf. 19:9), showing the seriousness with which they viewed this teaching.

The offer to live in shalom was not an insignificant matter to be shrugged off lightly. It was not offered in a carefree, take-it-or-leave-it attitude. These were choices for life and death, as the woes and warnings which conclude the passage make painfully clear. People need to know that the sentence for spurning such a direct, personal offer of forgiveness is so heavy that the judgments of Tyre and Sidon don't compare.

Thus the seventy were told to lay responsibility firmly on the consciences of those who refuse. Such are to be aware forever that they had seen the reality of God's shalom and turned it down. The opportunity for life had been at hand. They made their decision, and they will have to exist eternally with that choice of continuing alienation and insubordination.

> He who listens to you listens to me; he who rejects you rejects me.
> *Luke 10:16, NIV.*

That is the power of the emissary, which is why the appeal needs to be made so clearly, pointedly, and concretely. The reason Jesus took such care to instruct his followers about their spirit and methods is because life-and-death decisions rest on their witness. If the invitation is rejected due to the offensive attitudes or compromising actions of the missionaries, it is possible that it was not the shalom of God that has been spurned at all.

No wonder Jesus was so concerned for a complete, holistic, and integrated mission strategy. He wanted no contradiction between life, service, and message. J. C. Hoekendijk, in searching for a more biblical evangelism, made this interesting synopsis of shalom in Christ's ministry:

1. Shalom is proclaimed:
   the *kerygma* makes it a present offer.
2. Shalom is lived:
   the *koinonia* makes it reality here and now.
3. Shalom is demonstrated:
   the *diakonia* makes it visible to others.[4]

His concern was that missions today keep all three aspects in balance as Jesus did, so the message of shalom is heard, felt, and seen. Only then is our mission authentically biblical.

11

A Mission Shaped by Shalom

*T*he spread of Christian faith within a few years after the Luke 10 instructions were given indicates how authentic and effective the model was. How can we do the same in the mission settings of the 1980s? Since shalom beckons us to dream new thoughts and stir new hopes, we need to do it in the spirit of shalom. Like Martin Luther King, we dream of a new day while gazing on the promise of God's Spirit still bringing that vision to fulfillment. The reality of the God movement is always at hand.

Actually, this is not the only thing that impels us to dream. The setting in which that vision must be actualized in our world presses us either to dream or to despair. This planet speeds toward the twenty-first century with two critical graph-lines headed for collision: bulging populations and diminishing resources. We are seeing the early skirmishes and preparations for the worldwide finale in the struggle for survival. How else can one explain the madness of the armament races, while possibly twenty million people slowly starve in unbelievable conditions? Already in 1983 one estimate was that one billion people were suffering from hunger and malnutrition.[1]

Now is the time for the Jeremiahs of today to buy a field and plant a vineyard (Jeremiah 32:6ff.). Our children, growing up with little hope in a future threatened by nuclear annihilation, need a new vision of God's saving power amid that overwhelming crisis of need, fear, and violence. We do not need a head-in-the-sand escapism or a false faith that says God will never let it happen to us; we need instead an action-hope centered on a living Lord who continues to use a faithful remnant to accomplish shalom on earth. God will raise up someone to be faithful to the vision.

The question really is this: Can the God of shalom count on us? Whatever our analysis of the present or scenario of the future, an obvious need is to reconceptualize the mission task in terms of world needs and crises. Myriads of silent voices call for a strategy offering true hope and concrete alternatives. So let's dream of a mission to meet the challenge with the following shalom guidelines.

Mission Through Identification

A shalom-mission frees us to dream anew of the power of incarnation. We have seen that the biblical portrait of the good life in both Testaments was tied directly to a God who dwells among a responding people. The God-with-us event in Jesus of Nazareth unleashed the explosive enthusiasm in Acts, spreading the faith through the Roman world.

We need the power of an Emmanuel conviction. The church in mission is to be the visible presence of God in our cities and communities. Do we truly see ourselves as Christ's body, carrying on the same ministry of wholeness-making? We are to live, serve, and proclaim in Christ's stead. With the Spirit of God dwelling in us, we are more than representatives; we embody the divine presence as we extend that offer of shalom![2]

The reluctance of some missions to take the power of presence seriously reflects negatively on the doctrine of incarnation, whatever their creedal statements. Such attitudes and strategies seem to suggest that God really did not need to come and live with us. We dare not belittle the power of the verbal message, but if this can carry the freight alone, then God went to a lot of needless humiliation and suffering.

Historically the church in its mission has argued and vacillated between an emphasis on word and deed. Volumes have been written on the controversy. Perhaps a fresh appreciation for the concept of incarnational presence in mission will release us from the hassles and distortions of this agelong dichotomy. Both the "word-ers" and the "deed-ers" have ignored the foundational element of living: an authentic manifestation giving credence to both word and deed.

The shalom-mission calls for a full-orbed witness. An effective communication of the God-movement requires a balanced interaction between being, doing, and speaking. While none are adequate by themselves, the activities of preaching and serving are most meaningful when they flow naturally out of a living, open presence. God's love and truth are best seen and heard when "made flesh" in the daily life of someone who has "become one of them." Is not such deliberate identification what mission, as defined by God's own example, is all about? Is there any mission apart from the self-emptying of a former life and taking on the life of those to whom the witness is to be made? Anything less than such solidarity does not have the ring of integrity that the mission of God requires.

At the World Congress on Evangelism in Berlin John Stott declared:

> I personally believe that our failure to obey the implications of this command (As the Father sent me into the world, so send I you) is the greatest weakness of evangelical Christians in the field of evangelism today. We do not identify. We believe so strongly (and rightly) in proclamation, that we tend to proclaim our message from a distance. We sometimes appear like people who shout advice to drowning men from the safety of the seashore. We do not dive in to rescue them. We are afraid of getting wet, and indeed of greater perils than this. But Jesus Christ did not broadcast salvation from the sky. He visited us in great humility.[3]

Are we serious enough about our mission or about salvation itself to get that radical and costly? A burning desire for shalom on earth could give birth to some more strange and wonderful incarnations. Lonely outcasts and battered victims will again see God as one of them: female, black, Asian, slum-dweller, refugee, prisoner:

... I was hungry and you gave me food, ... I was sick and you visited me, ... I was in prison and you came to me.

Matthew 25:34ff.

Where can one find a more vivid portrayal of the shalom-mission? The Lord asks for nothing that we can't understand or do. The miracle which the Spirit seeks is the God-with-us transformation that enables us to be a brother or sister to every person longing for a true friend. Shalom begins when I open myself to another.

Is that too costly a dream, too revolutionary an idea to unleash on the world? What a change would occur if the church took its participation and solidarity in the human situation that seriously! With more authoritarian governments of left and right ideologies restricting or banning usual mission activities among many peoples of the world, we must rethink our mission. The surprise of Western Christians on discovering a healthy, growing church in China indicates our need to come to grips with a new day.

This is a good reminder that God is not tied to us or to our perceptions. The Holy Spirit will burst forth in new ways that relate to new realities. The most predictable thing about the God of shalom is the unpredictability. That calls for seeing visions and dreaming dreams (Acts 2:17). Is not that our sign that God's Spirit is at work?

Mission Through Community

We have learned that shalom is supremely relational. It weaves a web of commitments that creates the sense of mutuality and loyalty among those reaching out to each other. Can any more powerful image of mission be projected? Inherent in such experiences of community is the anticipation of the goal of the divine mission. "I will live in them and move among them" was Paul's summary of Yahweh's refrain through the prophets (2 Corinthians 6:16).

The purpose of reaching out to the lost and alienated ones is to welcome them into companionship. As we stand in God's stead offering forgiveness and showing acceptance, we form community where none had existed. Yet as we picture the persons who need this shalom the most, the prospect is no more pleasant or attractive for us than for God. Only the divine agape-love can create that new humanity among us.

That is the objective of both shalom and mission. But such lofty ideals can become reality only where persons truly meet in the nitty-gritty of life. Incarnations take place in smelly stable mangers and in humble towel-and-basin servanthood. Reconciliations and acceptance cannot be experienced in isolation or declared from the sky. They must be mediated person to person. Only Christ's body can incarnate God's shalom in a world that has never known real forgiveness or community.

The relationship of community and missions is stated intriguingly in the prophets' oracle by the peoples of the nations saying to Israel:

> Come, let us go up to the mountain of the Lord,
> . . . that he may teach us his ways
> and we may walk in his paths.
> Isaiah 2:3; Micah 4:2.

Mission is most captivating and compelling when the messenger and the receptor see themselves linking arms on a joint pilgrimage up God's mountain. Mission has no greater integrity than when the missionary and the new believer submit together in binding covenant to the rule of God.

That is what shalom-missions will do. How much more powerful will be our witness to unbelieving neighbors if we put our glib talk about "one-beggar-to-another" evangelism into actual spirit. Can we Western missionaries live without airs of superiority, viewing ourselves as learning-failing-forgiven-growing disciples like those we are leading to faith?

Such genuine participation in the good news will stimulate the same enthusiastic fellowship as described in Acts. We all struggle to allow the mission walls to be broken down and to interact as people who are "human like you," as Paul and Barnabas did at Lystra when treated as gods (Acts 14:15, NIV). To accept just a little honor and extra respect for all our sacrifice is such a temptation. On the other hand, Paul and Barnabas soon learned that the risk of appearing human can get one stoned to death. So much for not living up to expectations!

When Jesus sent the seventy to go and extend shalom, he was asking them to enter into a commitment of community with the people. If the divine purpose in history is to form a people of God, then mission is inviting others to experience that peoplehood with us. Shalom-mission reaches out to others and welcomes them to join in God's family, with all the feelings of belonging, security, and joy that family means.

I have a dream that missions will recapture this community-through-covenant as their primary goal *and* strategy. The words "Come, let us go up together" will ring out as the missionary commitment of full participation in the life of the people. Ephesians 2 will become a living reality amid every sphere of tension and strife on the globe—including Vietnam.

Is that an impossible dream? To what greater agenda can the church of the 1980s give itself in a world filled with confusion, fear, fighting, and famine? Our calling is to be God's authentic community and to reach out to every person wanting to experience that vision of shalom. What else is of ultimate importance for the people of God?

Mission Through Mutuality

A mission shaped by shalom will once again enjoy the contagious spirit of jubilee. Is anything more exhilarating than generous hearts responding to needs and hurts in true compassion? The jubilant spirit of sharing moves in quiet, spontaneous caring within this new community, not in patronizing handouts or demeaning charity drives. Such loving concern will also find a way to receive a gift in return.

This is not an attempt to clone the Jerusalem communal experience. Yet we have seen that shalom cannot be found in any group where abundant resources and desperate needs coexist in a state of indifference. It's a contradiction of terms. Servants of a Master who is jubilant in mercy, forgiveness, and favor will find ways to reflect that same spirit of generosity to other servants in need.

But a major cause of the paralysis that grips the Western church and missions is simply that this gap is so overwhelming. Recent studies from the U.S. Census Bureau indicate that male graduates from high school today will on the average each earn over a million dollars in their lifetime. (And they will likely struggle the entire time with pressing payments, feeling they need every cent to satisfy their needs without ever getting ahead.) How will that suburbanite hooked on American consumption ever relate meaningfully to just one of the 20,000,000 persons struggling to keep alive? Or to the countless millions more who feel chained in poverty, oppression, and despair?

This is a growing dilemma that engulfs us all. Any Westerner who retains even a semblance of the comfortable lifestyle to which we are accustomed simply cannot identify with the deprived masses. This immediately associates us, in most other countries, with the upper classes, who are viewed as the oppressors. Even when we make obvious sacrifices, everyone "knows" that we have a direct pipeline to the land of superabundance, where we will return when we are too worn out or sickly to continue.

The gap is great, and is getting greater. We all know that the earth does not have enough resources to provide a U.S.-middle-class-suburban standard of living for each of its billions of people. It is plain to many others, at least, that our comfort means their loss. The defense needed to keep it secure and to maintain its supplies is a tightening noose at our nation's throat. All this continues despite many sincere efforts in the past decade to reduce our tragic waste of nonrenewable resources and return to a simplified lifestyle.

We are trapped in multinational systems, technological worlds, and consumer-oriented societies that tend to force everyone to keep up or drop out entirely. Once again, regardless of our differing analyses or solutions, the North-South economic crisis is one that North American missions cannot continue to ignore. The hard questions are going to become more critical no matter what minor adjustments we make. By our very presence we are seen as having access to and accountability for vast resources.

This is precisely the context in which we are called to express that spirit of jubilee, promised by our Lord to every follower as part of the good news. Unless we begin censoring passages of the Gospels (Matthew 6:31-33; Mark 10:29-30; Luke 12:32-34), those who respond to our message have a right to expect something in the area of economic sharing. To spiritualize all of Christ's concerns and teachings in economics is surely one form of censoring the Scriptures.

Whatever the specific nature of our identification or the concrete shape of our community, we must work at this problem openly and purposefully. We need to allow the dynamics of our incarnation and participation to find ways to work out a spirit of mutuality. The Spirit forming the new community will enable this to happen without causing paternalism in the giver or dependence in the receiver. Rather, both the self-esteem *and* respect-for-the-other will be enhanced for each party.

An impossible dream? Then this biblical vision is only a hoax; either God is a liar or this mission is a failure. That New Testament portrait of a universal peoplehood rising above racial, social, and political interests to attain a fellowship where none has too much bread and none has too little is a cruel illusion. And we should stop talking about our covenant relationships and God's agape-love encompassing all people.

No, this dream insists that shalom will help us find ways to invite our neighbors into our vineyard. We don't need to be utopian in trying to achieve a universal equality or to reach the millions of needy ones. But shalom does give some specific principles for pooling local resources in ways that stretch them further by allowing the total group to live more self-sufficiently.

Isn't that how the Lord's promises to Peter of "100 times

more" were fulfilled? There was no manna from heaven, but there were a lot of jubilee celebrants freely sharing what they had. Today some Christian intentional communities and house church fellowships around the world are committed to working out this vision. But Christianity in general has appeared quite paralyzed in grappling with the economic realities in which missions are involved.

Missions could be doing so much more in the underdeveloped nations if we were seriously preaching the kingdom as Jesus did. We could find ways and means to bring healing and well-being in the lives and homes of those to whom we minister, not in the old forms of impersonal institutions, but in the glow of warm, caring friends reaching out to each other. That is not an impossible dream—hard, yes, but quite possible with God.

Mission Through Justice

This is the fourth element of a mission motivated by shalom. A compassionate caring for others will compel us to confront the powers that foster and maintain the anti-shalom of our world. The hard realism and astute politics discerned in Jesus' strategy will need to characterize his messengers today. It will also require the same powerful combination of boldness and meekness.

Missions facing the twenty-first century cannot afford the naivete and presumed innocence that allowed us to mask our confused identities and mixed roles in the past. The record of our Vietnam experience serves as a fitting example of missions' dilemma in the power-politics of our world. An American missionary who may have claimed to be apolitical in South Vietnam during the 1960s forfeits both credibility and respect.

This is probably the area where we suffer most from a hangover of colonial mentality. A missioner crossing national boundaries must relate to governments. The need for visas does foster a host-guest relationship which places us in particular situations which cannot be ignored. But that should not mean that we close our eyes to the systemic evil of nations and societies. The gospel message must not be sanitized of its leaven, light, and salt that express God's continuing concern for justice for all peoples of the world.

God's missionary cry, "Let my people go," needs to ring out wherever tyranny, oppression, and idolatry exist. We must learn to apply Romans 12 *and* 13 to all governments—right, center, and left—and pronounce to any power that opposes such loyalty the Lord's demand for primary allegiance. We tend to expect this where governments openly threaten the church, but we keep silent where they covertly use the church. Will we acknowledge that God's mission is highly political, placing every power and relationship under the same judgment and call?

A glance at the turmoil and confusion in such areas as Central America, the Middle East, South Africa, and Central Europe confirms that the relationships between missions and governments are not the simple, clean-cut associations that were assumed in the past. Signs point to greater disorder and complexity in the future, with more loyalties to clash and more violent pressure to conform. The political sphere with its multiple power structures will require far more careful attention and constant analysis for effective, long-term missions in the times ahead.

This does not necessarily mean increased involvement in the political structures. My study of Jesus' methods and the approach of the shalom community is pushing me currently towards less direct connections. But we are called to awareness and astuteness. Studies in political science and economics are as critical for today's missionary as those in anthropology, theology, and hermeneutics.

Here is where the shalom perspectives of the ministry and stance of Jesus are so helpful. One cannot walk a tighter rope than he walked between the clashing of Roman and Jewish systems and aspirations. The proof is in his ability to appeal to both sides. He was able to attract positive response from both the occupying centurions and the resisting guerrillas. His band of disciples included the sold-out tax-collector and the rebel Zealot. Conversely, it took collaboration by the establishment on both sides to bring about his death.

Yet Jesus never compromised his own position, which allowed him to speak to all groups, including "that fox" Herod (Luke 13:32; perhaps a more correct translation in our idiom today would be "that skunk"). He steadfastly refused to be involved with the tactics of violent destruction of either side. Rather, he taught and lived "a more excellent way" to deal with conflict and differences.

Nevertheless, Jesus died as a rebel. Though he could maintain a separate identity which allowed him to appeal to both sides, no one doubted where his sympathies rested and his compassion reached out. He stood with the disenfranchised, the poor, and the outcast and was literally "numbered with the transgressors" (Isaiah 53:12). His defiance before the high priest *and* the governor uttered the same silent cry of judgment to both: "Let my people go."

I dream of a day when missions will again be characterized by shalom's holy disturbance. Missionaries will more boldly confront whatever systems and policies oppose God's will for all people. We will be shaped by that shalom image of an angry Jesus stirring fear and hatred in the hearts of those whose power-base of false shalom was being broken up. The world needs more demonstrations of the passion and zeal for justice that seemed to devour the prince of shalom (John 2:17).

Missionaries today are hardly known for turning the world upside-down (or right-side-up) as were our predecessors (Acts 17:6). Nor are we known for political neutrality which would permit us to witness to the anti-shalom of all powers and ideologies that claim and demand too much. Is it unrealistic to look for the politics of Jesus in missions today?

A shalom missiology will at least sharpen the political realities and the issues of justice we must face. It will not supply ready answers, but it will serve as a guidepost pointing to the direction in which to move. It will prompt us to keep our priorities and attitudes more closely tuned to God's own heartbeat. The eternal and universal one dwelling among us will not be limited by our tribal or national interests.

Mission Through Suffering

The closing scene of this vision for mission concludes as Christ's own vision did. For all its wild dreams, vibrant aspirations, and explosive hopes, the nature of shalom leads to suffering. As with the closely related theme of redemption, no true shalom can exist in our setting apart from hurt and suffering. Given the facts of our selfish natures and a God-rejecting world, our dreaming of the good life must be done within the shadow of the cross.

Again we ask, Why should it be any different for us than it has been for God in the divine mission of restoring shalom? Jesus insisted that a disciple ought not think of him- or herself as being above the teacher. He said the household would be even more maligned than the master of the house (Matthew 10:24, 25). The way of suffering love is such an integral part of redemption that there simply cannot be any good news apart from it.

How can forgiveness and reconciliation exist without the willingness to pay the price by suffering loss and hurt? Anyone can retaliate, but only the God of agape-love and mercy is able to forgive and restore broken relationships. There will never be a shalom community for us if we are unable likewise to bear the pain and privation involved in offering to live in shalom.

That is why the vision of Eden will never be more than an impossible dream or a momentary longing for most people. We look at the price tag and walk away sadly. Only those willing to give up their own "shalom," with its false sense of security and prosperity, will find true shalom in Christ and others. This is the paradox of the seed needing to die if it is to live.

Jesus was speaking of his mission when he used this illustration of the seed (John 12:24). In our thought the concepts of bearing witness and being martyred for one's faith are not directly linked. But in the New Testament worldview they were inseparable, as we noted from Peter's writings. Mission was unthinkable apart from the same readiness to suffer as was shown in the divine mission. The martyrs viewed their blood as bearing new life in the body of Christ. They were participating in redemption history.

In contrast, the experience in Vietnam calls all missions today to come to grips with an existential understanding of the cross. We need not only to disassociate ourselves from the causes of suffering; we need to be ready to participate in the suffering of this world. Such a stance is identification *par excellence*. It identifies us as the lambs of God and the children of shalom.

This may sound as though a "martyr complex" is a missionary requirement, or it may sound like we are joining with Thomas in his moan: "Let us also go, that we may die with him" (John 11:16). As suggested from my anxiety recounted in the Prologue, suffering or death have no special merit of themselves. No blessing is gained by taking unnecessary risk, failing to use good judgment, or needlessly offending someone. Christians do bring suffering upon themselves for reasons that have little to do with God's mission.

We are speaking of suffering that is incurred by standing in Christ's stead. The clause, "for my sake and the gospel's" (Mark 8:35), makes our cross-bearing redemptive and purposeful. The effect of the witness on others and the glory given to the Lord from our lives result directly from the testimony that is heard and seen through the experience of suffering.

For us to appreciate the strength of meekness and the courage of vulnerability is hard. Our image of macho or bully power, resorting to physical force and violence to get its way, is a real obstacle to perceiving how God works. We find it difficult to believe that the merciful person who suffers is stronger and more influential than the one who retaliates with force (except for Jesus, who is seen as totally different). Yet even Jesus in his willingness to suffer was exercising faith in God's purposes: "but he trusted to him who judges justly" (1 Peter 2:23).

To maintain a healthy mind and spirit, we cannot emphasize suffering in isolation from the other dimensions of shalom in this chapter. Equally important, this stance is not normally to be taken by a lone individual. The redemptive witness through suffering should be the culmination of the entire community's presence, covenant, sharing, and witness. Only in such a unified and holistic confrontation of all evil and terror can we rejoice in hope and triumph amid our sufferings, as we are urged to do (Matthew 5:12; 1 Peter 4:13).

Is it too much to dream that missions would again be known for their willingness to suffer for the truth? I even dream of a broadened missionary version of the World Peace Pledge.[4] What a bold declaration of the meaning of faith that would be to our world in the 1980s. What a change such a proclamation would make in our image and identification. Are we ready to tell the world that we will seek to live by the way of the cross as we follow God's vision of shalom?

The World Mission Pledge

**In the light of mission of God who has called me,
I am prepared to live in shalom,
which I offer in the spirit of Christ.
to whomever I can share God's love.**

EPILOGUE

*I*n putting the finishing touches to this vision of our mission of tomorrow, I want to point to a sixth aspect of shalom that is an underlying motif in all the others. A shalom people is a pilgrim people. Or, to use New Testament imagery, we become aliens and exiles, strangers and pilgrims, passing through this world while searching for "a homeland . . . a better country" (see Hebrews 11:13-16; 13:14; 1 Peter 2:11).

We will not do well in a shalom-mission until we have learned to travel more lightly in life. With all its concern for total well-being, including prosperity and security, shalom is ironically for pilgrims. It is the gift of God given only to those who have been freed from laying up treasures on earth. Shalom simply cannot be bought, inherited, or manipulated. It can only be received as God's reward to those who have pulled up their stakes like Abraham and walk by faith with Yahweh in faithfulness.

One of the most fascinating expressions of the shalom-mission is the appeal Jeremiah wrote to God's people when they were exiled in Babylon:

> But seek the *shalom* of the city where I have sent you into exile, and pray to the Lord on its behalf, for in its *shalom* you will find your *shalom (29:7).*

The similarity of this text with the approach of Jesus in Luke 10 is remarkable. Jesus really changed only one word in his instructions to the seventy; they were being sent into mission rather than exile. Yet even that is mostly semantics; the main difference is that the disciples were forsaking homes and going to the turf of strangers by voluntary response. So exile for Israel meant mission, and mission for the seventy meant exile.

The need for lighter baggage in life applies as much to the social sphere as to the material. Our cultural heritage and superiority seem to cause as many barriers as our technology and lifestyles. Can we give up being so American? Can we give up being American, period? Why are so few willing even to consider changing citizenship—burning their bridges behind them and throwing their lot in with the community, society, and nation to which God has called them—to become immigrants, pioneers, and refugees?

Such thoughts put the priorities of the kingdom in painfully sharp confrontation. The prospect of making life a true pilgrimage forces us to face some tough issues regarding our trust, loyalties, and commitments. The question has not changed from when the prophets asked it of Israel or Jesus of the Jewish leaders: What is the source and basis of our shalom? Are we willing to be pilgrims and sojourners for the sake of God's rule and the universal mission of Christ?

The appeal to us is to seek wholeheartedly the shalom of the cities and lands where the Lord of the harvest wants us to be. The call is just as urgent in the inner cities of our own urban centers as across the seas. Wherever there are cries and brokenness because of the evil and selfishness of anti-shalom, God is looking for a shalom-loving person who will go there to live, to serve, and to say, "SHALOM!"

> Now may the Lord of *shalom* himself give you *shalom* at all times in all ways. The Lord be with you all.
>
> *2 Thessalonians 3:16.*

NOTES

Prologue

1. Ho Chi Minh City is the present name for the former "Pearl of the Orient." But I will use the geographical and political terminology that was used during the time period described.

2. Our neighbors said, "VC" (Viet Cong & Vietnamese Communist), which was a derogatory term for all Southerners with the opposition forces. I will use National Liberation Front, their own designation.

Chapter 1

1. Edward R. Dayton, ed., *Mission Handbook* (10th ed.), Monrovia, Calif.: MARC, 1973.

2. For affirmation of this, see the news interview in *The Alliance Witness*, December 17, 1975, p. 18.

3. Earl S. Martin, *Reaching the Other Side* (New York: Crown Publishers, Inc., 1978). Unfortunately, this "Journal of an American who stayed to witness Vietnam's postwar transition" has not been widely acclaimed in mission circles. His is a fascinating, well-written account of a revolutionary transition. It is a modern missionary story that missions would do well to ponder!

4. Since I start from a Christian pacifist position, my worldview will reflect certain sensitivities and values that may seem odd or stretched. I will try to be fair in my confronting, asking only that you hear the specific concerns in the context of the whole. While using some concrete examples, I have no personal rubs or records to set straight. We were all implicated and compromised.

5. Luke S. Martin, "An Evaluation of a Generation of Mennonite Mission, Service and Peacemaking in Vietnam, 1954-1976." This is an

unpublished paper, but a summary statement of it can be found in *Mission Focus: Current Issues*, Wilbert R. Shenk, ed. (Scottdale, Pa.: Herald Press, 1980), ch. 27. See also Martin's essay "Mennonites in Vietnam and God's New Creation" in *The Southeast Asia Journal of Theology* (Vol. 19, No. 1, 1978), pp. 42-51.

Chapter 2

1. Joseph Buttinger, *The Smaller Dragon* (New York: Frederick A. Praeger, Inc., 1858) carefully documents "the missionary cause" (p. 355) of the Society of Foreign Missions in Paris over a span of two full centuries. The campaign of plotting and pleading by their missionaries finally resulted in the conquest of Indochina by the French military in the 1850s (see pp. 222, 276, 304, and 338ff.).

2. See *Vietnam: Lotus in a Sea of Fire - A Buddhist Proposal for Peace* by Thich Nhat Hanh (New York: Hill and Wang, 1967), with foreword by Thomas Merton and afterword by Alfred Hassler (FOR). This voice representing the Buddhist majority was one of the most influential worldwide appeals in the anti-war movement. The powerful Buddhist resistance movement during the '60s would have been no surprise if we had known their history. It not only overturned several Saigon governments, it was a major force in the frustration of U.S. policy.

3. A good example of the attempt to rewrite the record is Guenter Lewy's *America in Vietnam* (New York: Oxford University Press, 1978). Lewy wants "to clear away the cobwebs of mythology that inhibit the correct understanding of what went on—and what went wrong—in Vietnam" (p. vi). His claim for doing this in his 540-page, closely documented volume is his first use of the U.S. military's classified records!

Chapter 3

1. Mrs. Gordon H. Smith, *Victory in Vietnam* (Grand Rapids: Zondervan Publishing House, 1965). A good way to grasp what I'm saying would be to read this book along with *Reaching the Other Side* (note 3 of chapter 1). Contrast the perceptions of the conflict expressed by both, and give special attention to the differences shown in hearing and appreciating all the people around them.

2. In the end, of course, that assessment was right. The key question for the military review might be, given the counter-effectiveness of the two wars and the foreigners increasingly trying to do the winning in both, if they ever really had a chance for success.

3. Even for those who wanted to relate to all Vietnamese equally, our need for logistics and for security caused all the church's assistance to support only the Saigon government. So the role of missions and relief

agencies in prolonging the conflict, thereby multiplying the very suffering we were trying to reduce, is a real and knotty issue.

4. It is noteworthy to record that some did hear our appeal that day. It stirred enough concern for several members of the commission to make a special trip with our friend, Don Luce, to the Con Son prison island. There they were finally able to "uncover" the Tiger Cages, an American-supported torture system that terrified all our student friends.

5. Robert F. Drinan, *Vietnam and Armageddon: Peace, War and the Christian Conscience* (New York: Sheed and Ward, 1970), ch. 7.

6. Op. cit., p. 167-8.

Chapter 4

1. Four members of IVS (International Voluntary Service) did resign and leave in protest. See Don Luce and John Sommer, *Vietnam: The Unheard Voices* (Ithaca, N.Y.: Cornell University Press, 1969) p. 20. While I was deeply moved by their action, it did not relieve my concern that a mission group take a stand—since IVS was not so seen.

2. Louis L. King, "The Sky Fell on Vietnam," *The Alliance Witness*, May 24, 1975, p. 17.

3. See the essay by James Klassen, "Walking with Vietnamese Christians"(*Mission Focus: Current Issues,* op.cit., Ch.26) for how one group did it.

4. Norman Kraus gives a similar example in *The Community of the Spirit* (Grand Rapids: Eerdmans, 1974) footnote 11, pp. 95-96.

Chapter 5

1. "El Salvador 'Critical,' Says Missionary," *The Goshen News*, July 3, 1982, p. 2.

2. See my essay, "Vietnam: I Wouldn't Do It Again," *Mission Focus*, op. cit.

3. The critical problem here is that even to recognize the possibility of facing a different government—while the conflict rages—is suggesting that which likely is both illegal and unthinkable. To enable Christians to prepare for such a possibility requires utmost tact and courage.

Chapter 6

1. Walter Brueggemann, *Living Toward a Vision: Biblical Reflections on Shalom* (Philadelphia: United Church Press, 1976) p. 16.

2. Gerhard von Rad, "*Shalom* in the Old Testament" in G. Kittel, ed., *Theological Wordbook of the New Testament* (Grand Rapids: Eerdmans, 1965) p. 402.

3. This is the conclusion of Walter Eisenbeis in *A Study of the Root Sh-L-M in the Old Testament* (Chicago: The University of Chicago,

1966). This is an unpublished English translation of his German dissertation published in Berlin in 1969. I have decided to use an unfamiliar term (shalom) and pour meaning into it rather than struggle with a common word (peace) which has so many meanings that are foreign to Hebraic thought. I believe the church would do well to add *shalom* to *agape* and *koinonia* as biblical terms with no English equivalents for our times. For further clarity on the distinctions of *shalom/eirēnē/pax* see Kraus, op. cit., p. 68ff., and John Driver, *Community and Commitment* (Scottdale: Herald Press, 1976) p. 72ff.

4. There is wide agreement among biblical scholars that the New Testament uses *eirēnē* with the sense of the Hebraic *shalom*, often reflecting a phrase or setting from the Old Testament. In his essay, "Politics and Peace in Luke's Gospel," Willard Swartley concludes that Luke "inherited meanings for *eirēnē* in Israel's multifaceted use of shalom ... [and that] the larger pervasive emphases of Luke's Gospel support a justice-shalom interpretation of Luke's *eirēnē"—Political Issues in Luke-Acts*, edited by Richard J. Cassidy and Philip I. Scharper (Maryknoll, N.Y.: Orbis Books, 1983) p. 34. Likewise, Norman Kraus says, "the 'gospel of peace' is the gospel of *shalom*, and not the gospel of the Greek *eirēnē* or the Roman *pax"* (op. cit., p. 69). See also Chapter 5 in John Driver's *Community and Commitment.*

Chapter 7

1. I am indebted to the Shalom Curriculum materials from the Joint Educational Development by United Church Press in Philadelphia: Edward A. Powers, *Signs of Shalom*, 1973; Hugh C. White, *Shalom in the Old Testament*, 1973; Paul L. Hammer, *Shalom in the New Testament*, 1973.

2. For the association of salvation and shalom, see Johannes Blauw, *The Missionary Nature of the Church* (Grand Rapids: Eerdmans, 1974). Blauw says, "the word 'salvation' in the Old Testament is a rendering of the word *shalom"* p. 53.

3. Johannes Pedersen, *Israel: Its Life and Culture* (England: Oxford University Press, 1926) pp. 263ff.

4. Charles C. West, "Reconciliation and World Peace" in *Reconciliation in Today's World*, Allen O. Miller, ed. (Grand Rapids: Eerdmans, 1969), p. 108.

5. Isaiah 56:3-8 is a good example of how the Law (Deuteronomy 23:1ff.) could be reinterpreted as a new setting called for a fresh vision of Yahweh's intention. It is no surprise that this is the missionary text that Jesus identified with when he opened the temple—see Matthew 21:12, 13 and especially 14.

6. See Exodus 21:22-25; Leviticus 24:19, 20; and Matthew 5:38. Hugh White's study is especially helpful on this subject.

7. Op. cit., p. 12.

Chapter 8

1. See Millard Lind, *Biblical Foundations for Christian Worship* (Scottdale: Herald Press, 1973) for this perspective.

2. Further documentation for this perspective can be found in Chapter 4, John H. Yoder, *The Politics of Jesus* (Grand Rapids: Eerdmans, 1972), and Millard C. Lind, *Yahweh Is a Warrior* (Scottdale: Herald Press, 1980).

3. See 1 Samuel 13:7ff. and 15:10ff. for the association of Gilgal with the new kingship.

4. This is the view of George E. Mendenhall, who writes, "The Old Testament Constantine, King David, represents a thoroughgoing reassimilation to Late Bronze Age religious ideas and structures." *The Tenth Generation* (Baltimore: The Johns Hopkins University Press, 1973), pp. 16, 17.

5. It is fascinating to observe in the Scriptures that the forces of evil also desire order—only they use the opposite means to achieve it. The use of force to attain order—power over people—is distinctly different from God's use of response and commitment—power by people.

6. John Bright, *A History of Israel* (Philadelphia: The Westminster Press, 1959), p. 328.

7. In a way, with the focus on God's kingship, Matthew 4:17 takes up where 1 Samuel 8:7 leaves off.

8. I will use the dynamic concept of this term, in agreement with Norman Kraus' definition: "The 'Kingdom of God' means God's saving, ruling presence." *The Community of the Spirit*, op. cit., p. 32.

9. Note that Stephen devotes twenty-four verses to the ministry of Moses, but only one factual sentence to David. Clearly, the politics and power of shalom are the most difficult to understand. The fact that many Christians still believe that God is doing in the Middle East today what the prophets rejected as God's will already in the Old Testament shows that even the Son has not been entirely successful in identifying the mission. How can we rightly fulfill our mission if we aren't clear on what God is about?

10. See Luke 9:57-62; 14:25-33 for reflection on the nature of covenant decisions.

11. William Klassen, "The Novel Element in the Love Commandment of Jesus" in *The New Way of Jesus*, William Klassen, ed. (Newton, Kan.: Faith and Life Press), p. 111.

12. The other leading New Testament character had similar struggles to learn this truth. Paul also thought at one time that force was needed in God's work (Acts 7:58; 22:4; 26:9ff.). But when he understood "this Way," he appealed: "Overcome evil with good ... never avenge yourselves, but leave it to the wrath of God" (Romans 12:17-21). See also 2 Corinthians 10:4 and Ephesians 6:12.

13. As though writing a special word for Americans, Peter affirms that it is fine to love and enjoy freedom if you have it, but Christians are not to allow that "right" to be the excuse for doing evil (1 Peter 2:16).

14. See chapter two of John H. Yoder, *Politics of Jesus,* op. cit.

Chapter 9

1. *Politics of Jesus,* op. cit. p. 66.

2. See Donald B. Kraybill, "Free Slaves," chapter 5 in *The Upside-Down Kingdom* (Scottdale: Herald Press, 1978).

3. John Driver has a fine development of this idea in chapter 2, "A Community of Sharing," op. cit.

4. Kraus' insights on this subject in *The Community of the Spirit* are helpful and provoking, pp. 55ff., 73ff., op. cit. See also Kraus, *The Authentic Witness* (Grand Rapids: Eerdmans, 1979), pp. 183 ff.

5. A helpful treatise on this subject is Marlin Jeschke's *Discipling the Brother* (Scottdale: Herald Press, 1973).

6. First Corinthians 7:15; 14:33 are two different settings where the principles of shalom were appealed to as giving specific guidelines for problems in daily life.

Chapter 10

1. I will use the designation "the seventy" for the group without commenting on the uncertainty of whether it was seventy or seventy-two persons. For our purposes it is more important to note that Matthew records most of the same instructions as given to the Twelve for their mission (10:1—11:1), which makes the passage even more of a paradigm for missions.

2. For documentation of Christianity's firm stance for the first three centuries see Roland H. Bainton, "The Pacifism of the Early Church," chapter 5 in *Christian Attitudes Toward War and Peace* (Nashville: Abingdon, 1960).

3. Werner Foerster, "*Eirēnē* in the New Testament," *Theological Dictionary of the New Testament,* Gerhard Kittel, ed., Vol. II, op. cit., p. 413.

4. J. C. Hoekendijk, *The Church Inside Out* (Philadelphia: The Westminster Press, 1964) p. 25.

Chapter 11

1. Reported at the United Nations-chartered World Food Council in their annual meeting for 1983.

2. John M. Perkins of "Voice of Calvary" is a current missioner whose dynamic concept of the incarnation in mission has led to an exciting work in Mississippi. See *With Justice for All* (Ventura, Calif.: Regal Books, 1982).

3. Quoted by Samuel Escobar, in *Is Revolution Change?* Brian Griffiths, ed. (Downers Grove, Ill.: Inter-Varsity Press, 1972), pp. 89-90.

4. The wording of the World Peace Pledge is, "In light of my faith, I am prepared to live without nuclear weapons in my country."

James E. Metzler was born on a Lancaster County (Pa.) farm in 1935, the second of five boys. His pilgrimage in mission began at age thirteen when Paul and Martha moved their family to Alabama to assist in new church planting efforts. Following several years of church work intertwined with college, Jim was ordained for missionary service with Eastern Mennonite Board of Missions in 1962.

Jim and Rachel (Gehman) served in Vietnam during the height of the American involvement (1962-70). They then transferred to the Philippines with Brian and Karen who had joined their family in Saigon. Jim began a new work in leadership training and economic development among independent churches in Luzon.

Following the termination of their Philippine ministry in 1976, Jim received an M.A. in Peace Studies degree from Associated Mennonite Biblical Seminaries. His thesis "Shalom and Mission," written under the supervision of John H. Yoder, became the foundational study for this book.

For the next five years Jim was the executive director of the Laurelville Mennonite Church Center near Pittsburgh, Pa. In 1982 the Metzlers located in Goshen, Ind., where Rachel is a nurse at Greencroft Nursing Center and Jim is admissions counselor at AMBS. Since 1979 he has served also on the board of directors of the Mennonite Board of Missions.

Missionary Study Series

Published by Herald Press, Scottdale, Pennsylvania, in association with the Institute of Mennonite Studies, Elkhart, Indiana.

1. *The Challenge of Church Growth.* A symposium edited by Wilbert R. Shenk with contributions also from John H. Yoder, Allan H. Howe, Robert L. Ramseyer, and J. Stanley Friesen (1973).

2. *Modern Messianic Movements, As a Theological and Missionary Challenge* by Gottfried Oosterwal (1973).

3. *From Kuku Hill: Among Indigenous Churches in West Africa* by Edwin and Irene Weaver (1975).

4. *Bibliography of Henry Venn's Printed Writings with Index* by Wilbert R. Shenk (1975).

5. *Christian Mission and Social Justice* by Samuel Escobar and John Driver (1978).

6. *A Spirituality of the Road* by David J. Bosch (1979).

7. *Mission and the Peace Witness: The Gospel and Christian Discipleship.* A symposium edited by Robert L. Ramseyer with contributions also from James E. Metzler, Marlin E. Miller, Richard Showalter, Ronald J. Sider, Sjouke Voolstra, and John H. Yoder (1979).

8. *Letters Concerning the Spread of the Gospel in the Heathen World* by Samuel S. Haury (1981).

9. *Evangelizing Neopagan North America* by Alfred C. Krass (1982).

10. *Anabaptism and Mission* edited by Wilbert R. Shenk (1984) with chapters by Franklin H. Littell, Cornelius J. Dyck, John H. Yoder, Hans Kasdorf, Wolfgang Schäufele, H. W. Meihuizen, Leonard Gross, N. van der Zijpp, José Gallardo, Wilbert R. Shenk, Robert L. Ramseyer, Takashi Yamada, and David A. Shank.

11. *From Saigon to Shalom* by James E. Metzler (1985).

The Missionary Study Series grows out of the Mennonite Missionary Study Fellowship (MMSF) program. The MMSF is an informal fellowship of persons interested in Christian mission, meeting annually for a three-day conference on issues central to their task. It includes missionaries, mission board administrators, theologians, sociologists, and others. It is sponsored by the Institute of Mennonite Studies (IMS), 3003 Benham Avenue, Elkhart, IN 46517. Books in the series may be ordered from Provident Bookstores, 616 Walnut Avenue, Scottdale, PA 15683.